Air Fryer Cookbook UK 2023

1000 Days Affordable & Easy Recipes That Anyone Can Cook at Home

Edward B. Bailey

Contents

INTRODUCTION

Practice makes perfect, which rings truer than ever in the world of cooking. Whether you are following a recipe or creating one as you go, it can take a few inedible trials, some not-so-bad attempts, and a few almost-there to perfect a meal. The beauty in all of the practice is that, as you go along, you begin to develop personalized approaches to certain recipes. You get familiar with spices, find alternatives for some condiments, and create your special sauces to pair with some standard dishes. And at the end of the day, that's truly what makes cooking worth it!

In all your meals and recipes, one essential aspect that can never be overlooked is having the right appliances to execute the instructions. If a recipe calls for broiling, an appliance for boiling will not deliver the same results. Similarly, if a recipe requires baking, grilling may lead the meal in an opposite direction. As a result, identifying and correctly interpreting your recipe is only one step in the perfection of your plated meal. A level of familiarity with the required appliances, and, of course, the latest technology in the available options of said appliances, becomes essential.

With the lessons and creations from my experience, I have curated a comprehensive guideline. From breaking down the technology to highlighting the best recipes for an air fryer, this cookbook is going to take you on a learning path. I have dedicated my time and experimented with tons of tricks and tips in my bid to ensure that this cookbook provides accurate and valid information on all you need to know about an appliance that should definitely be on your counter -an air fryer.

I hope you make great memories with this cookbook.

Enjoy Your Cooking!

Chapter 1 Air Fryer: Satisfy All Your Cooking Needs

Chapter 1 Air Fryer: Satisfy All Your Cooking Needs

From fast French fries to crispy chicken wings and mozzarella sticks, air fryers are a kitchen appliance that has gained viral spurts of popularity. However, while the name suggests a 'fryer,' this must-have appliance does not fry food items in the traditional concept of heated oil cooking. An air fryer operates like a convection oven, except that it is more portable, high-tech, and of course, more versatile in the context of meals. It is a three-part appliance with multiple controls that uses a convection-style heating element and a powerful fan to evenly spread heat to cook or crisp meals.

Choose a Right Air Fryer

Selecting the perfect choice depends on a few factors that are mostly related to personal preference.

Space and Capacity

You can get air fryers with standard baskets, which typically make two servings, or go as high as 2XL or 3XL, which are the larger air fryers that can make meals for up to six people at a time. However, while the number of people you tend to regularly cook for is the first pointer, the space you have is also a nudge in the right direction. You will get the right air fryer if you choose one based on the available space on your kitchen counter and the number of people you feed.

Controls

Air fryers with manual controls require you to twist the temperature and timer buttons to start the air fryer while the digital control has push buttons and, typically, more settings than manual control. If you want a standard air fryer that does the basics, you can stick with a manual control air fryer, but if you need an air fryer that can also serve as a toaster, oven, or pressure cooker, a digital air fryer is your best bet.

Ease of Cleaning

Most air fryers have a dishwasher-friendly base and basket, which makes them easy to clean after use. You should look out for those types of air fryers when selecting yours, because the options that have a more complex structure may be more difficult to clean.

Price

Ultimately, your budget is the final decision-maker for an air fryer. While I don't advise that you

skimp out on any kitchen appliance, so you can get the best from the best, I also understand that you need to be disciplined with a budget. Look out for air fryers that fit your budget and provide excellent quality.

General Tips for Cooking with Air Fryer

Cooking with an air fryer is exciting, fast, and easy. Here are a few tips to help you get started.

Preheat your air fryer like an oven

Air fryers operate with convection heating elements but, to get the best result from your meal, it is advisable to preheat your air fryer. Just like an oven, preheating your air fryer ensures that the food starts cooking immediately as the hot air is already circulated in the air fryer basket.

Less is more when it comes to oil in an air fryer

Unlike a deep fryer or pan-frying, an air fryer doesn't need large oils to be heated before the food cooks. As a matter of fact, when you have too much oil in the air fryer basket, it drops into the base and can cause your air fryer to emit tons of smoke or cause a mess during and after your cooking. You only need a light coat of oil on the food cooking in an air fryer.

Don't overcrowd your air fryer basket

Although air fryers come in different capacities, it is important not to maximize the size of your air fryer basket. When cooking in an air fryer, you need to ensure that the hot air can circulate adequately, which means you need to leave enough room in the air fryer basket for the food to evenly cook.

Shake the basket a couple of times for even browning

The heating element in an air fryer is typically located at the top of the appliance and the paired fan is what circulates the heat around the basket. If you don't flip the food in the basket or shake it around, you may end up with one side overcooked or undercooked. It is best to shake your air fryer basket a couple of times while cooking to make sure your food cooks evenly.

Advanced Air Fryer Tips and Tricks

Air fryers are capable of delivering more than crispy fries. Check out some advanced tips for making tasty meals with your air fryer.

Steaks and Pork: Flip for Even Browning

To cook steak in an air fryer, you can either marinate the meat in your preferred spices for a while or shortly before cooking. The number one thing to keep in mind, however, is that you need to flip the steak in 5 - 8 minutes intervals to ensure that it browns evenly. Although it may require close watching, the result will be a delicious and juicy steak, so it is definitely worth the wait.

Fish and Seafood: Avoid Overcrowding to Prevent Steam

The number one enemy of fish and seafood in an air fryer is steam, as it can make the food more wet than crispy. A simple way to prevent that pile of steam is to avoid overcrowding your air fryer basket when making seafood because more items in the basket mean that the circulating heat converts to steam. That way, you have more room in the basket to flip and bring your seafood to a crisp.

Chicken: Marinate for Extra Flavor

Air fryers can give you a tasty and crunchy chicken but, when you take the time to marinate your chicken for a bit longer (possibly overnight), you are rewarded with a burst of flavor in every bite. You can add oil to your marinade or use it as a final touch before putting the chicken in the air fryer basket. You can also use a dry coating or breading for an extra crunch.

Must-Have in Kitchen Pantry

An air fryer is an excellent way to shorten your cooking time and still get great results. To perfect the art of cooking with an air fryer, you need to pair your recipes with the right things from your pantry. Essentials to get you started include:

Oil and Vinegar

Always have your preferred type of oil, whether olive oil or coconut oil and a bottle of vinegar at hand for your meals. They are great for marinade and coating to bring out the flavor in your meat, seafood, and other dishes. Remember to avoid having a lot of liquid in your air fryer basket to prevent the base from burning with smoke.

Spices

The right spices can transform the taste of a meal and that's why you need to stay stocked up with all your favorite spices -and a few new ones, you never know what you may create.

Condiments

Condiments like ketchup, soy sauce, and soy sauce, are the final notes on a well-prepared meal and they can enhance the flavor you have carefully created. Never skimp out on your store-bought condiments and experiment with homemade condiments to find new tastes and transform your recipes.

Canned foods

Broth, sauces, and some vegetables are readily available in cans that add to the time-saving benefit of cooking with an air fryer. For longer shelf lives and less stressful meal preps, you should invest in canned foods for your kitchen pantry.

Dry foods

Pasta and rice are dry foods that must always be in your pantry, but you should consider more items like potatoes to have balanced meals that pair excellently with well-cooked meat and seafood from your air fryer.

With the manufacturer's manual, this cookbook guide, and a few ingredients, you can enjoy tasty meals with your air fryer.

Chapter 2 Breakfasts

Chapter 2 Breakfasts

Sausage Stuffed Peppers

Prep time: 15 minutes | Cook time: 15 minutes | Serves 4

230 g spicy pork sausage meat, removed from casings
4 large eggs
110 g full-fat cream cheese, softened
60 ml tinned diced tomatoes, drained
4 green peppers
8 tablespoons shredded chilli cheese
120 ml full-fat sour cream

1. In a medium skillet over medium heat, crumble and brown the sausage meat until no pink remains. Remove sausage and drain the fat from the pan. Crack eggs into the pan, scramble, and cook until no longer runny. 2. Place cooked sausage in a large bowl and fold in cream cheese. Mix in diced tomatoes. Gently fold in eggs. 3. Cut a 4-inch to 5-inch slit in the top of each pepper, removing the seeds and white membrane with a small knife. Separate the filling into four servings and spoon carefully into each pepper. Top each with 2 tablespoons cheese. 4. Place each pepper into the air fryer basket. 5. Adjust the temperature to 176°C and set the timer for 15 minutes. 6. Peppers will be soft and cheese will be browned when ready. Serve immediately with sour cream on top.

Pork Sausage Eggs with Mustard Sauce

Prep time: 20 minutes | Cook time: 12 minutes | Serves 8

450 g pork sausage meat
8 soft-boiled or hard-boiled eggs, peeled
1 large egg
2 tablespoons milk
235 ml crushed pork scratchings
Smoky Mustard Sauce:
60 ml mayonnaise
2 tablespoons sour cream
1 tablespoon Dijon mustard
1 teaspoon chipotle hot sauce

1. Preheat the air fryer to 200°C. 2. Divide the sausage into 8 portions. Take each portion of sausage, pat it down into a patty, and place 1 egg in the middle, gently wrapping the sausage around the egg until the egg is completely covered. (Wet your hands slightly if you find the sausage to be too sticky.) Repeat with the remaining eggs and sausage. 3. In a small shallow bowl, whisk the egg and milk until frothy. In another shallow bowl, place the crushed pork scratchings. Working one at a time, dip a sausage-wrapped egg into the beaten egg and then into the pork scratchings, gently rolling to coat evenly. Repeat with the remaining sausage-wrapped eggs. 4. Arrange the eggs in a single layer in the air fryer basket, and lightly spray with olive oil. Air fry for 10 to 12 minutes, pausing halfway through the baking time to turn the eggs, until the eggs are hot and the sausage is cooked through. 5. To make the sauce: In a small bowl, combine the mayonnaise, sour cream, Dijon, and hot sauce. Whisk until thoroughly combined. Serve with the Scotch eggs.

Cheddar Eggs

Prep time: 5 minutes | Cook time: 15 minutes | Serves 2

4 large eggs
2 tablespoons unsalted butter, melted
120 ml shredded sharp Cheddar cheese

1. Crack eggs into a round baking dish and whisk. Place dish into the air fryer basket. 2. Adjust the temperature to 204°C and set the timer for 10 minutes. 3. After 5 minutes, stir the eggs and add the butter and cheese. Let cook 3 more minutes and stir again. 4. Allow eggs to finish cooking an additional 2 minutes or remove if they are to your desired liking. 5. Use a fork to fluff. Serve warm.

Cauliflower Avocado Toast

Prep time: 15 minutes | Cook time: 8 minutes | Serves 2

1 (40 g) steamer bag cauliflower
1 large egg
120 ml shredded Mozzarella cheese
1 ripe medium avocado
½ teaspoon garlic powder
¼ teaspoon ground black pepper

1. Cook cauliflower according to package instructions. Remove from bag and place into cheesecloth or clean towel to remove excess moisture. 2. Place cauliflower into a large bowl and mix in egg and Mozzarella. Cut a piece of parchment to fit your air fryer basket. Separate the cauliflower mixture into two, and place it on the parchment in two mounds. Press out the cauliflower mounds into a ¼-inch-thick rectangle. Place the parchment into the air fryer basket. 3. Adjust the temperature to 204°C and set the timer for 8 minutes. 4. Flip the cauliflower halfway through the cooking time. 5. When the timer beeps, remove the parchment and allow the cauliflower to cool 5 minutes. 6. Cut open the avocado and remove the pit. Scoop out the inside, place it in a medium bowl, and mash it with garlic powder and pepper. Spread onto the cauliflower. Serve immediately.

Courgette Fritters

475 ml cooked spiralised or julienned courgette	60 ml blanched finely ground almond flour
2 tablespoons unsalted butter, softened	2 stalks spring onion, sliced
1 large egg	½ teaspoon garlic powder
	1 teaspoon dried parsley

1. Remove excess moisture from the courgette using a cheesecloth or kitchen towel. 2. Mix all ingredients in a large bowl. Form into four patties. 3. Cut a piece of parchment to fit your air fryer basket. Place each patty on the parchment and place into the air fryer basket. 4. Adjust the temperature to 204ºC and set the timer for 8 minutes. 5. Flip the patties halfway through the cooking time. Serve warm.

Strawberry Tarts

2 refrigerated piecrusts	30 g cream cheese, at room
120 ml strawberry preserves	temperature
1 teaspoon cornflour	3 tablespoons icing sugar
Cooking oil spray	Rainbow sprinkles, for
120 ml low-fat vanilla yoghurt	decorating

1. Place the piecrusts on a flat surface. Using a knife or pizza cutter, cut each piecrust into 3 rectangles, for 6 total. Discard any unused dough from the piecrust edges. 2. In a small bowl, stir together the preserves and cornflour. Mix well, ensuring there are no lumps of cornflour remaining. 3. Scoop 1 tablespoon of the strawberry mixture onto the top half of each piece of piecrust. 4. Fold the bottom of each piece up to enclose the filling. Using the back of a fork, press along the edges of each tart to seal. 5. Insert the crisper plate into the basket and the basket into the unit. Preheat the unit by selecting BAKE, setting the temperature to 192ºC, and setting the time to 3 minutes. Select START/STOP to begin. 6. Once the unit is preheated, spray the crisper plate with cooking oil. Working in batches, spray the breakfast tarts with cooking oil and place them into the basket in a single layer. Do not stack the tarts. 7. Select BAKE, set the temperature to 192ºC, and set the time to 10 minutes. Select START/STOP to begin. 8. When the cooking is complete, the tarts should be light golden brown. Let the breakfast tarts cool fully before removing them from the basket. 9. Repeat steps 5, 6, 7, and 8 for the remaining breakfast tarts. 10. In a small bowl, stir together the yoghurt, cream cheese, and icing sugar. Spread the breakfast tarts with the frosting and top with sprinkles.

Mushroom-and-Tomato Stuffed Hash Browns

Olive oil cooking spray	1 garlic clove, minced
1 tablespoon plus 2 teaspoons olive oil, divided	475 ml shredded potatoes
	½ teaspoon salt
110 g baby mushrooms, diced	¼ teaspoon black pepper
1 spring onion, white parts and green parts, diced	1 plum tomato, diced
	120 ml shredded mozzarella

1. Preheat the air fryer to 192ºC. Lightly coat the inside of a 6-inch cake pan with olive oil cooking spray. 2. In a small skillet, heat 2 teaspoons olive oil over medium heat. Add the mushrooms, spring onion, and garlic, and cook for 4 to 5 minutes, or until they have softened and are beginning to show some color. Remove from heat. 3. Meanwhile, in a large bowl, combine the potatoes, salt, pepper, and the remaining tablespoon olive oil. Toss until all potatoes are well coated. 4. Pour half of the potatoes into the bottom of the cake pan. Top with the mushroom mixture, tomato, and mozzarella. Spread the remaining potatoes over the top. 5. Bake in the air fryer for 12 to 15 minutes, or until the top is golden brown. 6. Remove from the air fryer and allow to cool for 5 minutes before slicing and serving.

Poached Eggs on Whole Grain Avocado Toast

Olive oil cooking spray	4 pieces wholegrain bread
4 large eggs	1 avocado
Salt	Red pepper flakes (optional)
Black pepper	

1. Preheat the air fryer to 160ºC. Lightly coat the inside of four small oven-safe ramekins with olive oil cooking spray. 2. Crack one egg into each ramekin, and season with salt and black pepper. 3. Place the ramekins into the air fryer basket. Close and set the timer to 7 minutes. 4. While the eggs are cooking, toast the bread in a toaster. 5. Slice the avocado in half lengthwise, remove the pit, and scoop the flesh into a small bowl. Season with salt, black pepper, and red pepper flakes, if desired. Using a fork, smash the avocado lightly. 6. Spread a quarter of the smashed avocado evenly over each slice of toast. 7. Remove the eggs from the air fryer, and gently spoon one onto each slice of avocado toast before serving.

Baked Egg and Mushroom Cups

Prep time: 5 minutes | Cook time: 15 minutes | Serves 6

Olive oil cooking spray
6 large eggs
1 garlic clove, minced
½ teaspoon salt
½ teaspoon black pepper

Pinch red pepper flakes
230 g baby mushrooms, sliced
235 ml fresh baby spinach
2 spring onions, white parts and green parts, diced

1. Preheat the air fryer to 160°C. Lightly coat the inside of six silicone muffin cups or a six-cup muffin tin with olive oil cooking spray. 2. In a large bowl, beat the eggs, garlic, salt, pepper, and red pepper flakes for 1 to 2 minutes, or until well combined. 3. Fold in the mushrooms, spinach, and spring onions. 4. Divide the mixture evenly among the muffin cups. 5. Place into the air fryer and bake for 12 to 15 minutes, or until the eggs are set. 6. Remove and allow to cool for 5 minutes before serving.

Fried Chicken Wings with Waffles

Prep time: 10 minutes | Cook time: 30 minutes | Serves 4

8 whole chicken wings
1 teaspoon garlic powder
Chicken seasoning, for preparing the chicken
Freshly ground black pepper, to taste

120 ml plain flour
Cooking oil spray
8 frozen waffles
Pure maple syrup, for serving (optional)

1. In a medium bowl, combine the chicken and garlic powder and season with chicken seasoning and pepper. Toss to coat. 2. Transfer the chicken to a resealable plastic bag and add the flour. Seal the bag and shake it to coat the chicken thoroughly. 3. Insert the crisper plate into the basket and the basket into the unit. Preheat the unit by selecting AIR FRY, setting the temperature to 204°C, and setting the time to 3 minutes. Select START/STOP to begin. 4. Once the unit is preheated, spray the crisper plate with cooking oil. Using tongs, transfer the chicken from the bag to the basket. It is okay to stack the chicken wings on top of each other. Spray them with cooking oil. 5. Select AIR FRY, set the temperature to 204°C, and set the time to 20 minutes. Select START/STOP to begin. 6. After 5 minutes, remove the basket and shake the wings. Reinsert the basket to resume cooking. Remove and shake the basket every 5 minutes until the chicken is fully cooked. 7. When the cooking is complete, remove the cooked chicken from the basket; cover to keep warm. 8. Rinse the basket and crisper plate with warm water. Insert them back into the unit. 9. Select AIR FRY, set the temperature to 182°C, and set the time to 3 minutes. Select START/STOP to begin. 10. Once the unit is preheated, spray the crisper plate with cooking spray. Working in batches, place the frozen waffles into the basket. Do not stack them. Spray the waffles with cooking oil. 11. Select AIR FRY, set the temperature to 182°C, and set the time to 6 minutes. Select START/STOP to begin. 12. When the cooking is complete, repeat steps 10 and 11 with the remaining waffles. 13. Serve the waffles with the chicken and a touch of maple syrup, if desired.

Greek Bagels

Prep time: 10 minutes | Cook time: 10 minutes | Makes 2 bagels

120 ml self-raising flour, plus more for dusting
120 ml plain Greek yoghurt
1 egg
1 tablespoon water

4 teaspoons sesame seeds or za'atar
Cooking oil spray
1 tablespoon butter, melted

1. In a large bowl, using a wooden spoon, stir together the flour and yoghurt until a tacky dough forms. Transfer the dough to a lightly floured work surface and roll the dough into a ball. 2. Cut the dough into 2 pieces and roll each piece into a log. Form each log into a bagel shape, pinching the ends together. 3. In a small bowl, whisk the egg and water. Brush the egg wash on the bagels. 4. Sprinkle 2 teaspoons of the toppings on each bagel and gently press it into the dough. 5. Insert the crisper plate into the basket and the basket into the unit. Preheat the unit by selecting BAKE, setting the temperature to 166°C, and setting the time to 3 minutes. Select START/STOP to begin. 6. Once the unit is preheated, spray the crisper plate with cooking spray. Drizzle the bagels with the butter and place them into the basket. 7. Select BAKE, set the temperature to 166°C, and set the time to 10 minutes. Select START/STOP to begin. 8. When the cooking is complete, the bagels should be lightly golden on the outside. Serve warm.

Breakfast Pitta

Prep time: 5 minutes | Cook time: 6 minutes | Serves 2

1 wholemeal pitta
2 teaspoons olive oil
½ shallot, diced
¼ teaspoon garlic, minced
1 large egg

¼ teaspoon dried oregano
¼ teaspoon dried thyme
⅛ teaspoon salt
2 tablespoons shredded Parmesan cheese

1. Preheat the air fryer to 192°C. 2. Brush the top of the pitta with olive oil, then spread the diced shallot and minced garlic over the pitta. 3. Crack the egg into a small bowl or ramekin, and season it with oregano, thyme, and salt. 4. Place the pitta into the air fryer basket, and gently pour the egg onto the top of the pitta. Sprinkle with cheese over the top. 5. Bake for 6 minutes. 6. Allow to cool for 5 minutes before cutting into pieces for serving.

Red Pepper and Feta Frittata

Prep time: 10 minutes | Cook time: 20 minutes | Serves 4

Olive oil cooking spray
8 large eggs
1 medium red pepper, diced
½ teaspoon salt

½ teaspoon black pepper
1 garlic clove, minced
120 ml feta, divided

1. Preheat the air fryer to 182°C. Lightly coat the inside of a 6-inch round cake pan with olive oil cooking spray. 2. In a large bowl, beat the eggs for 1 to 2 minutes, or until well combined. 3. Add the red pepper, salt, black pepper, and garlic to the eggs, and mix together until the red pepper is distributed throughout. 4. Fold in 60 ml the feta cheese. 5. Pour the egg mixture into the prepared cake pan, and sprinkle the remaining 60 ml feta over the top. 6. Place into the air fryer and bake for 18 to 20 minutes, or until the eggs are set in the center. 7. Remove from the air fryer and allow to cool for 5 minutes before serving.

Sirloin Steaks with Eggs

Prep time: 8 minutes | Cook time: 14 minutes per batch | Serves 4

Cooking oil spray
4 (110 g) sirloin steaks
1 teaspoon granulated garlic, divided
1 teaspoon salt, divided

1 teaspoon freshly ground black pepper, divided
4 eggs
½ teaspoon paprika

1. Insert the crisper plate into the basket and the basket into the unit. Preheat the unit by selecting AIR FRY, setting the temperature to 182°C, and setting the time to 3 minutes. Select START/STOP to begin. 2. Once the unit is preheated, spray the crisper plate with cooking oil. Place 2 steaks into the basket; do not oil or season them at this time. 3. Select AIR FRY, set the temperature to 182°C, and set the time to 9 minutes. Select START/STOP to begin. 4. After 5 minutes, open the unit and flip the steaks. Sprinkle each with ¼ teaspoon of granulated garlic, ¼ teaspoon of salt, and ¼ teaspoon of pepper. Resume cooking until the steaks register at least 64°C on a food thermometer. 5. When the cooking is complete, transfer the steaks to a plate and tent with aluminum foil to keep warm. Repeat steps 2, 3, and 4 with the remaining steaks. 6. Spray 4 ramekins with olive oil. Crack 1 egg into each ramekin. Sprinkle the eggs with the paprika and remaining ½ teaspoon each of salt and pepper. Working in batches, place 2 ramekins into the basket. 7. Select BAKE, set the temperature to 166°C, and set the time to 5 minutes. Select START/STOP to begin. 8. When the cooking is complete and the eggs are cooked to 72°C, remove the ramekins and repeat step 7 with the remaining 2 ramekins. 9. Serve the eggs with the steaks.

Baked Peach Oatmeal

Prep time: 5 minutes | Cook time: 30 minutes | Serves 6

Olive oil cooking spray
475 ml certified gluten-free rolled oats
475 ml unsweetened almond milk
60 ml honey, plus more for drizzling (optional)

120 ml non-fat plain Greek yoghurt
1 teaspoon vanilla extract
½ teaspoon ground cinnamon
¼ teaspoon salt
350 ml diced peaches, divided, plus more for serving (optional)

1. Preheat the air fryer to 192°C. Lightly coat the inside of a 6-inch cake pan with olive oil cooking spray. 2. In a large bowl, mix together the oats, almond milk, honey, yoghurt, vanilla, cinnamon, and salt until well combined. 3. Fold in 180 ml peaches and then pour the mixture into the prepared cake pan. 4. Sprinkle the remaining peaches across the top of the oatmeal mixture. Bake in the air fryer for 30 minutes. 5. Allow to set and cool for 5 minutes before serving with additional fresh fruit and honey for drizzling, if desired.

Honey-Apricot Granola with Greek Yoghurt

Prep time: 10 minutes | Cook time: 30 minutes | Serves 6

235 ml rolled oats
60 ml dried apricots, diced
60 ml almond slivers
60 ml walnuts, chopped
60 ml pumpkin seeds
60 to 80 ml honey, plus more for drizzling
1 tablespoon olive oil

1 teaspoon ground cinnamon
¼ teaspoon ground nutmeg
¼ teaspoon salt
2 tablespoons sugar-free dark chocolate chips (optional)
700 ml fat-free plain Greek yoghurt

1. Preheat the air fryer to 128°C. Line the air fryer basket with parchment paper. 2. In a large bowl, combine the oats, apricots, almonds, walnuts, pumpkin seeds, honey, olive oil, cinnamon, nutmeg, and salt, mixing so that the honey, oil, and spices are well distributed. 3. Pour the mixture onto the parchment paper and spread it into an even layer. 4. Bake for 10 minutes, then shake or stir and spread back out into an even layer. Continue baking for 10 minutes more, then repeat the process of shaking or stirring the mixture. Bake for an additional 10 minutes before removing from the air fryer. 5. Allow the granola to cool completely before stirring in the chocolate chips (if using) and pouring into an airtight container for storage. 6. For each serving, top 120 ml Greek yoghurt with 80 ml granola and a drizzle of honey, if needed.

Spinach and Swiss Frittata with Mushrooms

Prep time: 10 minutes | Cook time: 20 minutes | Serves 4

Olive oil cooking spray	110 g baby mushrooms, sliced
8 large eggs	1 shallot, diced
½ teaspoon salt	120 ml shredded Swiss cheese,
½ teaspoon black pepper	divided
1 garlic clove, minced	Hot sauce, for serving (optional)
475 ml fresh baby spinach	

1. Preheat the air fryer to 182ºC. Lightly coat the inside of a 6-inch round cake pan with olive oil cooking spray. 2. In a large bowl, beat the eggs, salt, pepper, and garlic for 1 to 2 minutes, or until well combined. 3. Fold in the spinach, mushrooms, shallot, and 60 ml the Swiss cheese. 4. Pour the egg mixture into the prepared cake pan, and sprinkle the remaining 60 ml Swiss over the top. 5. Place into the air fryer and bake for 18 to 20 minutes, or until the eggs are set in the center. 6. Remove from the air fryer and allow to cool for 5 minutes. Drizzle with hot sauce (if using) before serving.

Egg and Bacon Muffins

Prep time: 5 minutes | Cook time: 15 minutes | Serves 1

2 eggs	85 g shredded Cheddar cheese
Salt and ground black pepper, to	140 g cooked bacon
taste	1 spring onion, chopped
1 tablespoon green pesto	

1. Preheat the air fryer to 176ºC. Line a cupcake tin with parchment paper. 2. Beat the eggs with pepper, salt, and pesto in a bowl. Mix in the cheese. 3. Pour the eggs into the cupcake tin and top with the bacon and spring onion. 4. Bake in the preheated air fryer for 15 minutes, or until the egg is set. 5. Serve immediately.

Egg Tarts

Prep time: 10 minutes | Cook time: 17 to 20 minutes | Makes 2 tarts

⅓ sheet frozen puff pastry,	2 eggs
thawed	¼ teaspoon salt, divided
Cooking oil spray	1 teaspoon minced fresh parsley
120 ml shredded Cheddar	(optional)
cheese	

1. Insert the crisper plate into the basket and the basket into the unit. Preheat the unit by selecting BAKE, setting the temperature to 200ºC, and setting the time to 3 minutes. Select START/STOP to begin. 2. Lay the puff pastry sheet on a piece of parchment paper and cut it in half. 3. Once the unit is preheated, spray the crisper plate with cooking oil. Transfer the 2 squares of pastry to the basket, keeping them on the parchment paper. 4. Select BAKE, set the temperature to 200ºC, and set the time to 20 minutes. Select START/STOP to begin. 5. After 10 minutes, use a metal spoon to press down the center of each pastry square to make a well. Divide the cheese equally between the baked pastries. Carefully crack an egg on top of the cheese, and sprinkle each with the salt. Resume cooking for 7 to 10 minutes. 6. When the cooking is complete, the eggs will be cooked through. Sprinkle each with parsley (if using) and serve.

Bacon Cheese Egg with Avocado

Prep time: 15 minutes | Cook time: 20 minutes | Serves 4

6 large eggs	8 tablespoons full-fat sour
60 ml double cream	cream
350 ml chopped cauliflower	2 spring onions, sliced on the
235 ml shredded medium	bias
Cheddar cheese	12 slices bacon, cooked and
1 medium avocado, peeled and	crumbled
pitted	

1. In a medium bowl, whisk eggs and cream together. Pour into a round baking dish. 2. Add cauliflower and mix, then top with Cheddar. Place dish into the air fryer basket. 3. Adjust the temperature to 160ºC and set the timer for 20 minutes. 4. When completely cooked, eggs will be firm and cheese will be browned. Slice into four pieces. 5. Slice avocado and divide evenly among pieces. Top each piece with 2 tablespoons sour cream, sliced spring onions, and crumbled bacon.

Savory Sweet Potato Hash

Prep time: 15 minutes | Cook time: 18 minutes | Serves 6

2 medium sweet potatoes,	1 garlic clove, minced
peeled and cut into 1-inch cubes	½ teaspoon salt
½ green pepper, diced	½ teaspoon black pepper
½ red onion, diced	½ tablespoon chopped fresh
110 g baby mushrooms, diced	rosemary
2 tablespoons olive oil	

1.Preheat the air fryer to 192ºC. 2. In a large bowl, toss all ingredients together until the vegetables are well coated and seasonings distributed. 3. Pour the vegetables into the air fryer basket, making sure they are in a single even layer. (If using a smaller air fryer, you may need to do this in two batches.) 4. Roast for 9 minutes, then toss or flip the vegetables. Roast for 9 minutes more. 5. Transfer to a serving bowl or individual plates and enjoy.

Berry Muffins

Prep time: 15 minutes | Cook time: 12 to 17 minutes | Makes 8 muffins

315 ml plus 1 tablespoon plain flour, divided
60 ml granulated sugar
2 tablespoons light brown sugar
2 teaspoons baking powder

2 eggs
160 ml whole milk
80 ml neutral oil
235 ml mixed fresh berries

1. In a medium bowl, stir together 315 ml of flour, the granulated sugar, brown sugar, and baking powder until mixed well. 2. In a small bowl, whisk the eggs, milk, and oil until combined. Stir the egg mixture into the dry ingredients just until combined. 3. In another small bowl, toss the mixed berries with the remaining 1 tablespoon of flour until coated. Gently stir the berries into the batter. 4. Double up 16 foil muffin cups to make 8 cups. 5. Insert the crisper plate into the basket and the basket into the unit. Preheat the unit by selecting BAKE, setting the temperature to 156ºC, and setting the time to 3 minutes. Select START/STOP to begin. 6. Once the unit is preheated, place 1 L into the basket and fill each three-quarters full with the batter. 7. Select BAKE, set the temperature to 156ºC, and set the time for 17 minutes. Select START/STOP to begin. 8. After about 12 minutes, check the muffins. If they spring back when lightly touched with your finger, they are done. If not, resume cooking. 9. When the cooking is done, transfer the muffins to a wire rack to cool. 10. Repeat steps 6, 7, and 8 with the remaining muffin cups and batter. 11. Let the muffins cool for 10 minutes before serving.

White Bean–Oat Waffles

Prep time: 10 minutes | Cook time: 20 minutes | Serves 2

1 large egg white
2 tablespoons finely ground flaxseed
120 ml water
¼ teaspoon salt
1 teaspoon vanilla extract
120 ml cannellini beans, drained

and rinsed
1 teaspoon coconut oil
1 teaspoon liquid sweetener
120 ml old-fashioned rolled oats
Extra-virgin olive oil cooking spray

1. In a blender, combine the egg white, flaxseed, water, salt, vanilla, cannellini beans, coconut oil, and sweetener. Blend on high for 90 seconds. 2. Add the oats. Blend for 1 minute more. 3. Preheat the waffle iron. The batter will thicken to the correct consistency while the waffle iron preheats. 4. Spray the heated waffle iron with cooking spray. 5. Add 180 ml batter. Close the waffle iron. Cook for 6 to 8 minutes, or until done. Repeated with the remaining batter. 6. Serve hot, with your favorite sugar-free topping.

Wholemeal Banana-Walnut Bread

Prep time: 10 minutes | Cook time: 23 minutes | Serves 6

Olive oil cooking spray
2 ripe medium bananas
1 large egg
60 ml non-fat plain Greek yoghurt
60 ml olive oil
½ teaspoon vanilla extract

2 tablespoons honey
235 ml wholemeal flour
¼ teaspoon salt
¼ teaspoon baking soda
½ teaspoon ground cinnamon
60 ml chopped walnuts

1.Preheat the air fryer to 182ºC. Lightly coat the inside of a 8-by-4-inch loaf pan with olive oil cooking spray. (Or use two 5 ½-by-3-inch loaf pans.) 2. In a large bowl, mash the bananas with a fork. Add the egg, yoghurt, olive oil, vanilla, and honey. Mix until well combined and mostly smooth. 3. Sift the wholemeal flour, salt, baking soda, and cinnamon into the wet mixture, then stir until just combined. Do not overmix. 4. Gently fold in the walnuts. 5. Pour into the prepared loaf pan and spread to distribute evenly. 6. Place the loaf pan in the air fryer basket and bake for 20 to 23 minutes, or until golden brown on top and a toothpick inserted into the center comes out clean. 7. Allow to cool for 5 minutes before serving.

Maple Granola

Prep time: 5 minutes | Cook time: 40 minutes | Makes 475 ml

235 ml rolled oats
3 tablespoons pure maple syrup
1 tablespoon sugar
1 tablespoon neutral-flavored oil, such as refined coconut or

sunflower
¼ teaspoon sea salt
¼ teaspoon ground cinnamon
¼ teaspoon vanilla extract

1. Insert the crisper plate into the basket and the basket into the unit. Preheat the unit by selecting BAKE, setting the temperature to 120ºC, and setting the time to 3 minutes. Select START/STOP to begin. 2. In a medium bowl, stir together the oats, maple syrup, sugar, oil, salt, cinnamon, and vanilla until thoroughly combined. Transfer the granola to a 6-by-2-inch round baking pan. 3. Once the unit is preheated, place the pan into the basket. 4. Select BAKE, set the temperature to 120ºC and set the time to 40 minutes. Select START/STOP to begin. 5. After 10 minutes, stir the granola well. Resume cooking, stirring the granola every 10 minutes, for a total of 40 minutes, or until the granola is lightly browned and mostly dry. 6. When the cooking is complete, place the granola on a plate to cool. It will become crisp as it cools. Store the completely cooled granola in an airtight container in a cool, dry place for 1 to 2 weeks.

Blueberry Cobbler

80 ml wholemeal pastry flour

¾ teaspoon baking powder

Dash sea salt

120 ml semi-skimmed milk

2 tablespoons pure maple syrup

½ teaspoon vanilla extract

Cooking oil spray

120 ml fresh blueberries

60 ml granola

1. In a medium bowl, whisk the flour, baking powder, and salt. Add the milk, maple syrup, and vanilla and gently whisk, just until thoroughly combined. 2. Preheat the unit by selecting BAKE, setting the temperature to 176ºC, and setting the time to 3 minutes. Select START/STOP to begin. 3. Spray a 6-by-2-inch round baking pan with cooking oil and pour the batter into the pan. Top evenly with the blueberries and granola. 4. Once the unit is preheated, place the pan into the basket. 5. Select BAKE, set the temperature to 176ºC, and set the time to 15 minutes. Select START/STOP to begin. 6. When the cooking is complete, the cobbler should be nicely browned and a knife inserted into the middle should come out clean. Enjoy plain or topped with a little vanilla yoghurt.

Wholemeal Blueberry Muffins

Olive oil cooking spray

120 ml unsweetened applesauce

60 ml honey

120 ml non-fat plain Greek yoghurt

1 teaspoon vanilla extract

1 large egg

350 ml plus 1 tablespoon wholemeal, divided

½ teaspoon baking soda

½ teaspoon baking powder

½ teaspoon salt

120 ml blueberries, fresh or frozen

1.Preheat the air fryer to 182ºC. Lightly coat the inside of six silicone muffin cups or a six-cup muffin tin with olive oil cooking spray. 2. In a large bowl, combine the applesauce, honey, yoghurt, vanilla, and egg and mix until smooth. 3. Sift in 350 ml of the flour, the baking soda, baking powder, and salt into the wet mixture, then stir until just combined. 4. In a small bowl, toss the blueberries with the remaining 1 tablespoon flour, then fold the mixture into the muffin batter. 5. Divide the mixture evenly among the prepared muffin cups and place into the basket of the air fryer. Bake for 12 to 15 minutes, or until golden brown on top and a toothpick inserted into the middle of one of the muffins comes out clean. 6. Allow to cool for 5 minutes before serving.

Chapter 3 Poultry

Chapter 3 Poultry

Ham Chicken with Cheese

Prep time: 15 minutes | Cook time: 25 minutes | Serves 4

55 g unsalted butter, softened	60 ml water
115 g cream cheese, softened	280 g shredded cooked chicken
1½ teaspoons Dijon mustard	115 g ham, chopped
2 tablespoons white wine vinegar	115 g sliced Swiss or Provolone cheese

1. Preheat the air fryer to 190ºC. Lightly coat a casserole dish that will fit in the air fryer, such as an 8-inch round pan, with olive oil and set aside. 2. In a large bowl and using an electric mixer, combine the butter, cream cheese, Dijon mustard, and vinegar. With the motor running at low speed, slowly add the water and beat until smooth. Set aside. 3. Arrange an even layer of chicken in the bottom of the prepared pan, followed by the ham. Spread the butter and cream cheese mixture on top of the ham, followed by the cheese slices on the top layer. Air fry for 20 to 25 minutes until warmed through and the cheese has browned.

Classic Chicken Kebab

Prep time: 35 minutes | Cook time: 25 minutes | Serves 4

60 ml olive oil	450 g boneless skinless chicken thighs, cut into 1-inch pieces
1 teaspoon garlic powder	
1 teaspoon onion powder	1 red bell pepper, cut into 1-inch pieces
1 teaspoon ground cumin	
½ teaspoon dried oregano	1 red onion, cut into 1-inch pieces
½ teaspoon dried basil	
60 ml lemon juice	1 courgette, cut into 1-inch pieces
1 tablespoon apple cider vinegar	
Olive oil cooking spray	12 cherry tomatoes

1. In a large bowl, mix together the olive oil, garlic powder, onion powder, cumin, oregano, basil, lemon juice, and apple cider vinegar. 2. Spray six skewers with olive oil cooking spray. 3. On each skewer, slide on a piece of chicken, then a piece of bell pepper, onion, courgette, and finally a tomato and then repeat. Each skewer should have at least two pieces of each item. 4. Once all of the skewers are prepared, place them in a 9-by-13-inch baking dish and pour the olive oil marinade over the top of the skewers. Turn each skewer so that all sides of the chicken and vegetables are coated. 5. Cover the dish with plastic wrap and place it in the refrigerator for 30 minutes. 6. After 30 minutes, preheat the air fryer to 192ºC. (If using a grill attachment, make sure it is inside the air fryer during preheating.) 7. Remove the skewers from the marinade and lay them in a single layer in the air fryer basket. If the air fryer has a grill attachment, you can also lay them on this instead. 8. Cook for 10 minutes. Rotate the kebabs, then cook them for 15 minutes more. 9. Remove the skewers from the air fryer and let them rest for 5 minutes before serving.

Chicken Wings with Piri Piri Sauce

Prep time: 30 minutes | Cook time: 30 minutes | Serves 6

12 chicken wings	and chopped
45 g butter, melted	1 tablespoon pimiento, seeded and minced
1 teaspoon onion powder	
½ teaspoon cumin powder	1 garlic clove, chopped
1 teaspoon garlic paste	2 tablespoons fresh lemon juice
Sauce:	⅓ teaspoon sea salt
60 g piri piri peppers, stemmed	½ teaspoon tarragon

1. Steam the chicken wings using a steamer basket that is placed over a saucepan with boiling water; reduce the heat. 2. Now, steam the wings for 10 minutes over a moderate heat. Toss the wings with butter, onion powder, cumin powder, and garlic paste. 3. Let the chicken wings cool to room temperature. Then, refrigerate them for 45 to 50 minutes. 4. Roast in the preheated air fryer at 170ºC for 25 to 30 minutes; make sure to flip them halfway through. 5. While the chicken wings are cooking, prepare the sauce by mixing all of the sauce ingredients in a food processor. Toss the wings with prepared Piri Piri Sauce and serve.

Lemon-Basil Turkey Breasts

Prep time: 30 minutes | Cook time: 58 minutes | Serves 4

2 tablespoons olive oil	black pepper, to taste
900 g turkey breasts, bone-in, skin-on	1 teaspoon fresh basil leaves, chopped
Coarse sea salt and ground	2 tablespoons lemon zest, grated

1. Rub olive oil on all sides of the turkey breasts; sprinkle with salt, pepper, basil, and lemon zest. 2. Place the turkey breasts skin side up on the parchment-lined air fryer basket. 3. Cook in the preheated air fryer at 170ºC for 30 minutes. Now, turn them over and cook an additional 28 minutes. 4. Serve with lemon wedges, if desired. Bon appétit!

Chicken with Bacon and Tomato

Prep time: 25 minutes | Cook time: 10 minutes | Serves 4

4 medium-sized skin-on chicken drumsticks	2 tablespoons olive oil
1½ teaspoons herbs de Provence	2 garlic cloves, crushed
Salt and pepper, to taste	340 g crushed canned tomatoes
1 tablespoon rice vinegar	1 small-size leek, thinly sliced
	2 slices smoked bacon, chopped

1. Sprinkle the chicken drumsticks with herbs de Provence, salt and pepper; then, drizzle them with rice vinegar and olive oil. 2. Cook in the baking pan at 180ºC for 8 to 10 minutes. Pause the air fryer; stir in the remaining ingredients and continue to cook for 15 minutes longer; make sure to check them periodically. Bon appétit!

Coconut Chicken Wings with Mango Sauce

Prep time: 15 minutes | Cook time: 20 minutes | Serves 4

16 chicken drumettes (party wings)	coconut
60 ml full-fat coconut milk	60 g all-purpose flour
1 tablespoon sriracha	Cooking oil spray
1 teaspoon onion powder	165 g mango, cut into ½-inch chunks
1 teaspoon garlic powder	15 g fresh coriander, chopped
Salt and freshly ground black pepper, to taste	25 g red onion, chopped
25 g shredded unsweetened	2 garlic cloves, minced
	Juice of ½ lime

1. Place the drumettes in a resealable plastic bag. 2. In a small bowl, whisk the coconut milk and sriracha. 3. Drizzle the drumettes with the sriracha–coconut milk mixture. Season the drumettes with the onion powder, garlic powder, salt, and pepper. Seal the bag. Shake it thoroughly to combine the seasonings and coat the chicken. Marinate for at least 30 minutes, preferably overnight, in the refrigerator. 4. When the drumettes are almost done marinating, in a large bowl, stir together the shredded coconut and flour. 5. Dip the drumettes into the coconut-flour mixture. Press the flour mixture onto the chicken with your hands. 6. Insert the crisper plate into the basket and the basket into the unit. Preheat the unit by selecting AIR FRY, setting the temperature to 200ºC, and setting the time to 3 minutes. Select START/STOP to begin. 7. Once the unit is preheated, spray the crisper plate and the basket with cooking oil. Place the drumettes in the air fryer. It is okay to stack them. Spray the drumettes with cooking oil, being sure to cover the bottom layer. 8. Select AIR FRY, set the temperature to 200ºC, and set the time to 20 minutes. Select START/STOP to begin. 9. After 5 minutes, remove the basket and shake it to ensure all pieces cook through. Reinsert the basket to resume cooking. Remove and shake the basket every 5 minutes, twice more, until a food thermometer inserted into the drumettes registers 76ºC. 10. When the cooking is complete, let the chicken cool for 5 minutes. 11. While the chicken cooks and cools, make the salsa. In a small bowl, combine the mango, coriander, red onion, garlic, and lime juice. Mix well until fully combined. Serve with the wings.

Chicken Legs with Leeks

Prep time: 30 minutes | Cook time: 18 minutes | Serves 6

2 leeks, sliced	skinless
2 large-sized tomatoes, chopped	½ teaspoon smoked cayenne pepper
3 cloves garlic, minced	
½ teaspoon dried oregano	2 tablespoons olive oil
6 chicken legs, boneless and	A freshly ground nutmeg

1. In a mixing dish, thoroughly combine all ingredients, minus the leeks. Place in the refrigerator and let it marinate overnight. 2. Lay the leeks onto the bottom of the air fryer basket. Top with the chicken legs. 3. Roast chicken legs at (190ºC for 18 minutes, turning halfway through. Serve with hoisin sauce.

Golden Tenders

Prep time: 10 minutes | Cook time: 15 minutes | Serves 4

120 g panko bread crumbs	pepper
1 tablespoon paprika	16 chicken tenders
½ teaspoon salt	115 g mayonnaise
¼ teaspoon freshly ground black	Olive oil spray

1. In a medium bowl, stir together the panko, paprika, salt, and pepper. 2. In a large bowl, toss together the chicken tenders and mayonnaise to coat. Transfer the coated chicken pieces to the bowl of seasoned panko and dredge to coat thoroughly. Press the coating onto the chicken with your fingers. 3. Insert the crisper plate into the basket and the basket into the unit. Preheat the unit by selecting AIR FRY, setting the temperature to 180ºC, and setting the time to 3 minutes. Select START/STOP to begin. 4. Once the unit is preheated, place a parchment paper liner into the basket. Place the chicken into the basket and spray it with olive oil. 5. Select AIR FRY, set the temperature to 180ºC, and set the time to 15 minutes. Select START/STOP to begin. 6. When the cooking is complete, the tenders will be golden brown and a food thermometer inserted into the chicken should register 76ºC. For more even browning, remove the basket halfway through cooking and flip the tenders. Give them an extra spray of olive oil and reinsert the basket to resume cooking. This ensures they are crispy and brown all over. 7. When the cooking is complete, serve.

General Tso's Chicken

Prep time: 10 minutes | Cook time: 14 minutes | Serves 4

1 tablespoon sesame oil

1 teaspoon minced garlic

½ teaspoon ground ginger

240 ml chicken broth

4 tablespoons soy sauce, divided

½ teaspoon sriracha, plus more for serving

2 tablespoons hoisin sauce

4 tablespoons cornflour, divided

4 boneless, skinless chicken breasts, cut into 1-inch pieces

Olive oil spray

2 medium spring onions, sliced, green parts only

Sesame seeds, for garnish

1. In a small saucepan over low heat, combine the sesame oil, garlic, and ginger and cook for 1 minute. 2. Add the chicken broth, 2 tablespoons of soy sauce, the sriracha, and hoisin. Whisk to combine. 3. Whisk in 2 tablespoons of cornflour and continue cooking over low heat until the sauce starts to thicken, about 5 minutes. Remove the pan from the heat, cover it, and set aside. 4. Insert the crisper plate into the basket and the basket into the unit. Preheat the unit by selecting BAKE, setting the temperature to 200ºC, and setting the time to 3 minutes. Select START/STOP to begin. 5. In a medium bowl, toss together the chicken, remaining 2 tablespoons of soy sauce, and remaining 2 tablespoons of cornflour. 6. Once the unit is preheated, spray the crisper plate with olive oil. Place the chicken into the basket and spray it with olive oil. 7. Select BAKE, set the temperature to 200ºC, and set the time to 9 minutes. Select START/STOP to begin. 8. After 5 minutes, remove the basket, shake, and spray the chicken with more olive oil. Reinsert the basket to resume cooking. 9. When the cooking is complete, a food thermometer inserted into the chicken should register at least 76ºC. Transfer the chicken to a large bowl and toss it with the sauce. Garnish with the spring onions and sesame seeds and serve.

Italian Chicken with Sauce

Prep time: 15 minutes | Cook time: 20 minutes | Serves 4

2 large skinless chicken breasts (about 565 g)

Salt and freshly ground black pepper

50 g almond meal

45 g grated Parmesan cheese

2 teaspoons Italian seasoning

1 egg, lightly beaten

1 tablespoon olive oil

225 g no-sugar-added marinara sauce

4 slices Mozzarella cheese or 110 g shredded Mozzarella

1. Preheat the air fryer to 180ºC. 2. Slice the chicken breasts in half horizontally to create 4 thinner chicken breasts. Working with one piece at a time, place the chicken between two pieces of parchment paper and pound with a meat mallet or rolling pin to flatten to an even thickness. Season both sides with salt and freshly ground black pepper. 3. In a large shallow bowl, combine the almond meal, Parmesan, and Italian seasoning; stir until thoroughly combined. Place the egg in another large shallow bowl. 4. Dip the chicken in the egg, followed by the almond meal mixture, pressing the mixture firmly into the chicken to create an even coating. 5. Working in batches if necessary, arrange the chicken breasts in a single layer in the air fryer basket and coat both sides lightly with olive oil. Pausing halfway through the cooking time to flip the chicken, air fry for 15 minutes, or until a thermometer inserted into the thickest part registers 76ºC. 6. Spoon the marinara sauce over each piece of chicken and top with the Mozzarella cheese. Air fry for an additional 3 to 5 minutes until the cheese is melted.

Italian Crispy Chicken

Prep time: 10 minutes | Cook time: 20 minutes | Serves 4

2 (115 g) boneless, skinless chicken breasts

2 egg whites, beaten

120 g Italian bread crumbs

45 g grated Parmesan cheese

2 teaspoons Italian seasoning

Salt and freshly ground black pepper, to taste

Cooking oil spray

180 g marinara sauce

110 g shredded Mozzarella cheese

1. With your knife blade parallel to the cutting board, cut the chicken breasts in half horizontally to create 4 thin cutlets. On a solid surface, pound the cutlets to flatten them. You can use your hands, a rolling pin, a kitchen mallet, or a meat hammer. 2. Pour the egg whites into a bowl large enough to dip the chicken. 3. In another bowl large enough to dip a chicken cutlet in, stir together the bread crumbs, Parmesan cheese, and Italian seasoning, and season with salt and pepper. 4. Dip each cutlet into the egg whites and into the breadcrumb mixture to coat. 5. Insert the crisper plate into the basket and the basket into the unit. Preheat the unit by selecting AIR FRY, setting the temperature to 190ºC, and setting the time to 3 minutes. Select START/STOP to begin. 6. Once the unit is preheated, spray the crisper plate with cooking oil. Working in batches, place 2 chicken cutlets into the basket. Spray the top of the chicken with cooking oil. 7. Select AIR FRY, set the temperature to 190ºC, and set the time to 7 minutes. Select START/STOP to begin. 8. When the cooking is complete, repeat steps 6 and 7 with the remaining cutlets. 9. Top the chicken cutlets with the marinara sauce and shredded Mozzarella cheese. If the chicken will fit into the basket without stacking, you can prepare all 4 at once. Otherwise, do this 2 cutlets at a time. 10. Select AIR FRY, set the temperature to 190ºC, and set the time to 3 minutes. Select START/STOP to begin. 11. The cooking is complete when the cheese is melted and the chicken reaches an internal temperature of 76ºC. Cool for 5 minutes before serving.

Breaded Turkey Cutlets

Prep time: 5 minutes | Cook time: 8 minutes | Serves 4

60 g whole wheat bread crumbs	⅛ teaspoon garlic powder
¼ teaspoon paprika	1 egg
¼ teaspoon salt	4 turkey breast cutlets
¼ teaspoon black pepper	Chopped fresh parsley, for
⅛ teaspoon dried sage	serving

1. Preheat the air fryer to 192°C. 2. In a medium shallow bowl, whisk together the bread crumbs, paprika, salt, black pepper, sage, and garlic powder. 3. In a separate medium shallow bowl, whisk the egg until frothy. 4. Dip each turkey cutlet into the egg mixture, then into the bread crumb mixture, coating the outside with the crumbs. Place the breaded turkey cutlets in a single layer in the bottom of the air fryer basket, making sure that they don't touch each other. 5. Bake for 4 minutes. Turn the cutlets over, then bake for 4 minutes more, or until the internal temperature reaches 76°C. Sprinkle on the parsley and serve.

Buffalo Crispy Chicken Strips

Prep time: 15 minutes | Cook time: 13 to 17 minutes per batch | Serves 4

90 g all-purpose flour	pepper
2 eggs	16 chicken breast strips, or 3
2 tablespoons water	large boneless, skinless chicken
120 g seasoned panko bread	breasts, cut into 1-inch strips
crumbs	Olive oil spray
2 teaspoons granulated garlic	60 ml Buffalo sauce, plus more
1 teaspoon salt	as needed
1 teaspoon freshly ground black	

1. Put the flour in a small bowl. 2. In another small bowl, whisk the eggs and the water. 3. In a third bowl, stir together the panko, granulated garlic, salt, and pepper. 4. Dip each chicken strip in the flour, in the egg, and in the panko mixture to coat. Press the crumbs onto the chicken with your fingers. 5. Insert the crisper plate into the basket and the basket into the unit. Preheat the unit by selecting AIR FRY, setting the temperature to 190°C, and setting the time to 3 minutes. Select START/STOP to begin. 6. Once the unit is preheated, place a parchment paper liner into the basket. Working in batches if needed, place the chicken strips into the basket. Do not stack unless using a wire rack for the second layer. Spray the top of the chicken with olive oil. 7. Select AIR FRY, set the temperature to 190°C, and set the time to 17 minutes. Select START/STOP to begin. 8. After 10 or 12 minutes, remove the basket, flip the chicken, and spray again with olive oil. Reinsert the basket to resume cooking. 9. When the cooking is complete, the chicken should be golden brown and crispy and a food thermometer inserted

into the chicken should register 76°C. 10. Repeat steps 6, 7, and 8 with any remaining chicken. 11. Transfer the chicken to a large bowl. Drizzle the Buffalo sauce over the top of the cooked chicken, toss to coat, and serve.

Wild Rice and Kale Stuffed Chicken Thighs

Prep time: 10 minutes | Cook time: 22 minutes | Serves 4

4 boneless, skinless chicken	1 teaspoon salt
thighs	Juice of 1 lemon
250 g cooked wild rice	100 g crumbled feta
35 g chopped kale	Olive oil cooking spray
2 garlic cloves, minced	1 tablespoon olive oil

1. Preheat the air fryer to 192°C. 2. Place the chicken thighs between two pieces of plastic wrap, and using a meat mallet or a rolling pin, pound them out to about ¼-inch thick. 3. In a medium bowl, combine the rice, kale, garlic, salt, and lemon juice and mix well. 4. Place a quarter of the rice mixture into the middle of each chicken thigh, then sprinkle 2 tablespoons of feta over the filling. 5. Spray the air fryer basket with olive oil cooking spray. 6. Fold the sides of the chicken thigh over the filling, and then gently place each of them seam-side down into the air fryer basket. Brush each stuffed chicken thigh with olive oil. 7. Roast the stuffed chicken thighs for 12 minutes, then turn them over and cook for an additional 10 minutes, or until the internal temperature reaches 76°C.

Stuffed Turkey Roulade

Prep time: 10 minutes | Cook time: 45 minutes | Serves 4

1 (900 g) boneless turkey breast,	1 tablespoon fresh sage
skin removed	2 garlic cloves, minced
1 teaspoon salt	2 tablespoons olive oil
½ teaspoon black pepper	Fresh chopped parsley, for
115 g goat cheese	garnish
1 tablespoon fresh thyme	

1. Preheat the air fryer to 192°C. 2. Using a sharp knife, butterfly the turkey breast, and season both sides with salt and pepper and set aside. 3. In a small bowl, mix together the goat cheese, thyme, sage, and garlic. 4. Spread the cheese mixture over the turkey breast, then roll it up tightly, tucking the ends underneath. 5. Place the turkey breast roulade onto a piece of aluminum foil, wrap it up, and place it into the air fryer. 6. Bake for 30 minutes. Remove the foil from the turkey breast and brush the top with oil, then continue cooking for another 10 to 15 minutes, or until the outside has browned and the internal temperature reaches 76°C. 7. Remove and cut into 1-inch-wide slices and serve with a sprinkle of parsley on top.

Chicken and Gruyère Cordon Bleu

Prep time: 15 minutes | Cook time: 15 minutes | Serves 4

4 chicken breast filets	Freshly ground black pepper, to
75 g chopped ham	taste
75 g grated Swiss cheese, or	½ teaspoon dried marjoram
Gruyère cheese	1 egg
30 g all-purpose flour	120 g panko bread crumbs
Pinch salt	Olive oil spray

1. Put the chicken breast filets on a work surface and gently press them with the palm of your hand to make them a bit thinner. Don't tear the meat. 2. In a small bowl, combine the ham and cheese. Divide this mixture among the chicken filets. Wrap the chicken around the filling to enclose it, using toothpicks to hold the chicken together. 3. In a shallow bowl, stir together the flour, salt, pepper, and marjoram. 4. In another bowl, beat the egg. 5. Spread the panko on a plate. 6. Dip the chicken in the flour mixture, in the egg, and in the panko to coat thoroughly. Press the crumbs into the chicken so they stick well. 7. Insert the crisper plate into the basket and the basket into the unit. Preheat the unit by selecting BAKE, setting the temperature to 190ºC, and setting the time to 3 minutes. Select START/STOP to begin. 8. Once the unit is preheated, spray the crisper plate with olive oil. Place the chicken into the basket and spray it with olive oil. 9. Select BAKE, set the temperature to 190ºC, and set the time to 15 minutes. Select START/STOP to begin. 10. When the cooking is complete, the chicken should be cooked through and a food thermometer inserted into the chicken should register 76ºC. Carefully remove the toothpicks and serve.

Crisp Paprika Chicken Drumsticks

Prep time: 5 minutes | Cook time: 22 minutes | Serves 2

2 teaspoons paprika	4 (140 g) chicken drumsticks,
1 teaspoon packed brown sugar	trimmed
1 teaspoon garlic powder	1 teaspoon vegetable oil
½ teaspoon dry mustard	1 scallion, green part only,
½ teaspoon salt	sliced thin on bias
Pinch pepper	

1. Preheat the air fryer to 200ºC. 2. Combine paprika, sugar, garlic powder, mustard, salt, and pepper in a bowl. Pat drumsticks dry with paper towels. Using metal skewer, poke 10 to 15 holes in skin of each drumstick. Rub with oil and sprinkle evenly with spice mixture. 3. Arrange drumsticks in air fryer basket, spaced evenly apart, alternating ends. Air fry until chicken is crisp and registers 90ºC, 22 to 25 minutes, flipping chicken halfway through cooking. 4. Transfer chicken to serving platter, tent loosely with aluminum foil, and let rest for 5 minutes. Sprinkle with scallion and serve.

Piri-Piri Chicken Thighs

Prep time: 5 minutes | Cook time: 25 minutes | Serves 4

60 ml piri-piri sauce	1 tablespoon extra-virgin olive
1 tablespoon freshly squeezed	oil
lemon juice	4 bone-in, skin-on chicken
2 tablespoons brown sugar,	thighs, each weighing
divided	approximately 200 to 230 g
2 cloves garlic, minced	½ teaspoon cornflour

1. To make the marinade, whisk together the piri-piri sauce, lemon juice, 1 tablespoon of brown sugar, and the garlic in a small bowl. While whisking, slowly pour in the oil in a steady stream and continue to whisk until emulsified. Using a skewer, poke holes in the chicken thighs and place them in a small glass dish. Pour the marinade over the chicken and turn the thighs to coat them with the sauce. Cover the dish and refrigerate for at least 15 minutes and up to 1 hour. 2. Preheat the air fryer to 190ºC. Remove the chicken thighs from the dish, reserving the marinade, and place them skin-side down in the air fryer basket. Air fry until the internal temperature reaches 76ºC, 15 to 20 minutes. 3. Meanwhile, whisk the remaining brown sugar and the cornflour into the marinade and microwave it on high power for 1 minute until it is bubbling and thickened to a glaze. 4. Once the chicken is cooked, turn the thighs over and brush them with the glaze. Air fry for a few additional minutes until the glaze browns and begins to char in spots. 5. Remove the chicken to a platter and serve with additional piri-piri sauce, if desired.

Crunchy Chicken Tenders

Prep time: 5 minutes | Cook time: 12 minutes | Serves 4

1 egg	½ teaspoon dried thyme
60 ml unsweetened almond milk	½ teaspoon dried sage
30 g whole wheat flour	½ teaspoon garlic powder
30 g whole wheat bread crumbs	450 g chicken tenderloins
½ teaspoon salt	1 lemon, quartered
½ teaspoon black pepper	

1. Preheat the air fryer to 184ºC. 2. In a shallow bowl, beat together the egg and almond milk until frothy. 3. In a separate shallow bowl, whisk together the flour, bread crumbs, salt, pepper, thyme, sage, and garlic powder. 4. Dip each chicken tenderloin into the egg mixture, then into the bread crumb mixture, coating the outside with the crumbs. Place the breaded chicken tenderloins into the bottom of the air fryer basket in an even layer, making sure that they don't touch each other. 5. Cook for 6 minutes, then turn and cook for an additional 5 to 6 minutes. Serve with lemon slices.

Garlic Soy Chicken Thighs

Prep time: 10 minutes | Cook time: 30 minutes | Serves 1 to 2

2 tablespoons chicken stock
2 tablespoons reduced-sodium soy sauce
1½ tablespoons sugar
4 garlic cloves, smashed and peeled

2 large spring onions, cut into 2- to 3-inch batons, plus more, thinly sliced, for garnish
2 bone-in, skin-on chicken thighs (198 to 225 g each)

1. Preheat the air fryer to 190ºC. 2. In a metal cake pan, combine the chicken stock, soy sauce, and sugar and stir until the sugar dissolves. Add the garlic cloves, spring onions, and chicken thighs, turning the thighs to coat them in the marinade, then resting them skin-side up. Place the pan in the air fryer and bake, flipping the thighs every 5 minutes after the first 10 minutes, until the chicken is cooked through and the marinade is reduced to a sticky glaze over the chicken, about 30 minutes. 3. Remove the pan from the air fryer and serve the chicken thighs warm, with any remaining glaze spooned over top and sprinkled with more sliced spring onions.

Spicy Chicken Thighs and Gold Potatoes

Prep time: 5 minutes | Cook time: 25 minutes | Serves 4

4 bone-in, skin-on chicken thighs
½ teaspoon kosher salt or ¼ teaspoon fine salt
2 tablespoons melted unsalted butter
2 teaspoons Worcestershire sauce
2 teaspoons curry powder
1 teaspoon dried oregano leaves

½ teaspoon dry mustard
½ teaspoon granulated garlic
¼ teaspoon paprika
¼ teaspoon hot pepper sauce
Cooking oil spray
4 medium Yukon gold potatoes, chopped
1 tablespoon extra-virgin olive oil

1. Sprinkle the chicken thighs on both sides with salt. 2. In a medium bowl, stir together the melted butter, Worcestershire sauce, curry powder, oregano, dry mustard, granulated garlic, paprika, and hot pepper sauce. Add the thighs to the sauce and stir to coat. 3. Insert the crisper plate into the basket and the basket into the unit. Preheat the unit by selecting AIR FRY, setting the temperature to 200ºC, and setting the time to 3 minutes. Select START/STOP to begin. 4. Once the unit is preheated, spray the crisper plate with cooking oil. In the basket, combine the potatoes and olive oil and toss to coat. 5. Add the wire rack to the air fryer and place the chicken thighs on top. 6. Select AIR FRY, set the temperature to 200ºC, and set the time to 25 minutes. Select START/STOP to begin. 7. After 19 minutes check the chicken thighs. If a food thermometer inserted into the chicken registers 76ºC, transfer them to a clean plate, and cover with aluminum foil to keep warm. If they aren't cooked to 76ºC, resume cooking for another 1 to 2 minutes until they are done. Remove them from the unit along with the rack. 8. Remove the basket and shake it to distribute the potatoes. Reinsert the basket to resume cooking for 3 to 6 minutes, or until the potatoes are crisp and golden brown. 9. When the cooking is complete, serve the chicken with the potatoes.

Barbecue Chicken

Prep time: 10 minutes | Cook time: 18 to 20 minutes | Serves 4

60 ml no-salt-added tomato sauce
2 tablespoons low-sodium grainy mustard
2 tablespoons apple cider vinegar

1 tablespoon honey
2 garlic cloves, minced
1 jalapeño pepper, minced
3 tablespoons minced onion
4 (140 g) low-sodium boneless, skinless chicken breasts

1. Preheat the air fryer to 190ºC. 2. In a small bowl, stir together the tomato sauce, mustard, cider vinegar, honey, garlic, jalapeño, and onion. 3. Brush the chicken breasts with some sauce and air fry for 10 minutes. 4. Remove the air fryer basket and turn the chicken; brush with more sauce. Air fry for 5 minutes more. 5. Remove the air fryer basket and turn the chicken again; brush with more sauce. Air fry for 3 to 5 minutes more, or until the chicken reaches an internal temperature of 76ºC on a meat thermometer. Discard any remaining sauce. Serve immediately.

Chicken Burgers with Ham and Cheese

Prep time: 12 minutes | Cook time: 13 to 16 minutes | Serves 4

40 g soft bread crumbs
3 tablespoons milk
1 egg, beaten
½ teaspoon dried thyme
Pinch salt
Freshly ground black pepper, to

taste
570 g chicken mince
70 g finely chopped ham
75 g grated Gouda cheese
Olive oil for misting

1. Preheat the air fryer to 180ºC. 2. In a medium bowl, combine the bread crumbs, milk, egg, thyme, salt, and pepper. Add the chicken and mix gently but thoroughly with clean hands. 3. Form the chicken into eight thin patties and place on waxed paper. 4. Top four of the patties with the ham and cheese. Top with remaining four patties and gently press the edges together to seal, so the ham and cheese mixture is in the middle of the burger. 5. Place the burgers in the basket and mist with olive oil. Bake for 13 to 16 minutes or until the chicken is thoroughly cooked to 76ºC as measured with a meat thermometer. Serve immediately.

Jalapeño Chicken Balls

Prep time: 10 minutes | Cook time: 25 minutes | Serves 4

1 medium red onion, minced	3 tablespoons ground almonds
2 garlic cloves, minced	1 egg
1 jalapeño pepper, minced	1 teaspoon dried thyme
2 teaspoons extra-virgin olive oil	450 g chicken mince breast
	Cooking oil spray

1. Insert the crisper plate into the basket and the basket into the unit. Preheat the unit by selecting BAKE, setting the temperature to 200ºC, and setting the time to 3 minutes. Select START/STOP to begin. 2. In a 6-by-2-inch round pan, combine the red onion, garlic, jalapeño, and olive oil. 3. Once the unit is preheated, place the pan into the basket. 4. Select BAKE, set the temperature to 200ºC, and set the time to 4 minutes. Select START/STOP to begin. 5. When the cooking is complete, the vegetables should be crisp-tender. Transfer to a medium bowl. 6. Mix the almonds, egg, and thyme into the vegetable mixture. Add the chicken and mix until just combined. Form the chicken mixture into about 24 (1-inch) balls. 7. Insert the crisper plate into the basket and the basket into the unit. Preheat the unit by selecting BAKE, setting the temperature to 200ºC, and setting the time to 3 minutes. Select START/STOP to begin. 8. Once the unit is preheated, spray the crisper plate with cooking oil. Working in batches, place half the meatballs in a single layer, not touching, into the basket. 9. Select BAKE, set the temperature to 200ºC, and set the time to 10 minutes. Select START/STOP to begin. 10. When the cooking is complete, a food thermometer inserted into the meatballs should register at least 76ºC. 11. Repeat steps 8 and 9 with the remaining meatballs. Serve warm.

Barbecued Chicken with Creamy Coleslaw

Prep time: 10 minutes | Cook time: 20 minutes | Serves 2

270 g shredded coleslaw mix	plus extra for serving
Salt and pepper	2 tablespoons mayonnaise
2 (340 g) bone-in split chicken breasts, trimmed	2 tablespoons sour cream
1 teaspoon vegetable oil	1 teaspoon distilled white vinegar, plus extra for seasoning
2 tablespoons barbecue sauce,	¼ teaspoon sugar

1. Preheat the air fryer to 180ºC. 2. Toss coleslaw mix and ¼ teaspoon salt in a colander set over bowl. Let sit until wilted slightly, about 30 minutes. Rinse, drain, and dry well with a dish towel. 3. Meanwhile, pat chicken dry with paper towels, rub with oil, and season with salt and pepper. Arrange breasts skin-side down in air fryer basket, spaced evenly apart, alternating ends. Bake for 10 minutes. Flip breasts and brush skin side with barbecue sauce.

Return basket to air fryer and bake until well browned and chicken registers 70ºC, 10 to 15 minutes. 4. Transfer chicken to serving platter, tent loosely with aluminum foil, and let rest for 5 minutes. While chicken rests, whisk mayonnaise, sour cream, vinegar, sugar, and pinch pepper together in a large bowl. Stir in coleslaw mix and season with salt, pepper, and additional vinegar to taste. Serve chicken with coleslaw, passing extra barbecue sauce separately.

Thai Curry Meatballs

Prep time: 10 minutes | Cook time: 10 minutes | Serves 4

450 g chicken mince	1 tablespoon fish sauce
15 g chopped fresh coriander	2 garlic cloves, minced
1 teaspoon chopped fresh mint	2 teaspoons minced fresh ginger
1 tablespoon fresh lime juice	½ teaspoon kosher salt
1 tablespoon Thai red, green, or yellow curry paste	½ teaspoon black pepper
	¼ teaspoon red pepper flakes

1. Preheat the air fryer to 200ºC. 2. In a large bowl, gently mix the chicken mince, coriander, mint, lime juice, curry paste, fish sauce, garlic, ginger, salt, black pepper, and red pepper flakes until thoroughly combined. 3. Form the mixture into 16 meatballs. Place the meatballs in a single layer in the air fryer basket. Air fry for 10 minutes, turning the meatballs halfway through the cooking time. Use a meat thermometer to ensure the meatballs have reached an internal temperature of 76ºC. Serve immediately.

Yellow Curry Chicken Thighs with Peanuts

Prep time: 10 minutes | Cook time: 20 minutes | Serves 6

120 ml unsweetened full-fat coconut milk	1 tablespoon minced garlic
2 tablespoons yellow curry paste	1 teaspoon kosher salt
1 tablespoon minced fresh ginger	450 g boneless, skinless chicken thighs, halved crosswise
	2 tablespoons chopped peanuts

1. In a large bowl, stir together the coconut milk, curry paste, ginger, garlic, and salt until well blended. Add the chicken; toss well to coat. Marinate at room temperature for 30 minutes, or cover and refrigerate for up to 24 hours. 2. Preheat the air fryer to 190ºC. 3. Place the chicken (along with marinade) in a baking pan. Place the pan in the air fryer basket. Bake for 20 minutes, turning the chicken halfway through the cooking time. Use a meat thermometer to ensure the chicken has reached an internal temperature of 76ºC. 4. Sprinkle the chicken with the chopped peanuts and serve.

Cranberry Curry Chicken

Prep time: 12 minutes | Cook time: 18 minutes | Serves 4

3 (140 g) low-sodium boneless, skinless chicken breasts, cut into 1½-inch cubes
2 teaspoons olive oil
2 tablespoons cornflour
1 tablespoon curry powder
1 tart apple, chopped
120 ml low-sodium chicken broth
60 g dried cranberries
2 tablespoons freshly squeezed orange juice
Brown rice, cooked (optional)

1. Preheat the air fryer to 196°C. 2. In a medium bowl, mix the chicken and olive oil. Sprinkle with the cornflour and curry powder. Toss to coat. Stir in the apple and transfer to a metal pan. Bake in the air fryer for 8 minutes, stirring once during cooking. 3. Add the chicken broth, cranberries, and orange juice. Bake for about 10 minutes more, or until the sauce is slightly thickened and the chicken reaches an internal temperature of 76°C on a meat thermometer. Serve over hot cooked brown rice, if desired.

Israeli Chicken Schnitzel

Prep time: 5 minutes | Cook time: 10 minutes | Serves 4

2 large boneless, skinless chicken breasts, each weighing about 450 g
125 g all-purpose flour
2 teaspoons garlic powder
2 teaspoons kosher salt
1 teaspoon black pepper
1 teaspoon paprika
2 eggs beaten with 2 tablespoons water
250 g panko bread crumbs
Vegetable oil spray
Lemon juice, for serving

1. Preheat the air fryer to 190°C. 2. Place 1 chicken breast between 2 pieces of plastic wrap. Use a mallet or a rolling pin to pound the chicken until it is ¼ inch thick. Set aside. Repeat with the second breast. Whisk together the flour, garlic powder, salt, pepper, and paprika on a large plate. Place the panko in a separate shallow bowl or pie plate. 3. Dredge 1 chicken breast in the flour, shaking off any excess, then dip it in the egg mixture. Dredge the chicken breast in the panko, making sure to coat it completely. Shake off any excess panko. Place the battered chicken breast on a plate. Repeat with the second chicken breast. 4. Spray the air fryer basket with oil spray. Place 1 of the battered chicken breasts in the basket and spray the top with oil spray. Air fry until the top is browned, about 5 minutes. Flip the chicken and spray the second side with oil spray. Air fry until the second side is browned and crispy and the internal temperature reaches 76°C. Remove the first chicken breast from the air fryer and repeat with the second chicken breast. 5. Serve hot with lemon juice.

Celery Chicken

Prep time: 10 minutes | Cook time: 15 minutes | Serves 4
120 ml soy sauce
2 tablespoons hoisin sauce
4 teaspoons minced garlic
1 teaspoon freshly ground black pepper
8 boneless, skinless chicken tenderloins
120 g chopped celery
1 medium red bell pepper, diced
Olive oil spray

1. Preheat the air fryer to 190°C. Spray the air fryer basket lightly with olive oil spray. 2. In a large bowl, mix together the soy sauce, hoisin sauce, garlic, and black pepper to make a marinade. Add the chicken, celery, and bell pepper and toss to coat. 3. Shake the excess marinade off the chicken, place it and the vegetables in the air fryer basket, and lightly spray with olive oil spray. You may need to cook them in batches. Reserve the remaining marinade. 4. Air fry for 8 minutes. Turn the chicken over and brush with some of the remaining marinade. Air fry for an additional 5 to 7 minutes, or until the chicken reaches an internal temperature of at least 76°C. Serve.

Herb-Buttermilk Chicken Breast

Prep time: 5 minutes | Cook time: 40 minutes | Serves 2

1 large bone-in, skin-on chicken breast
240 ml buttermilk
1½ teaspoons dried parsley
1½ teaspoons dried chives
¾ teaspoon kosher salt
½ teaspoon dried dill
½ teaspoon onion powder
¼ teaspoon garlic powder
¼ teaspoon dried tarragon
Cooking spray

1. Place the chicken breast in a bowl and pour over the buttermilk, turning the chicken in it to make sure it's completely covered. Let the chicken stand at room temperature for at least 20 minutes or in the refrigerator for up to 4 hours. 2. Meanwhile, in a bowl, stir together the parsley, chives, salt, dill, onion powder, garlic powder, and tarragon. 3. Preheat the air fryer to 150°C. 4. Remove the chicken from the buttermilk, letting the excess drip off, then place the chicken skin-side up directly in the air fryer. Sprinkle the seasoning mix all over the top of the chicken breast, then let stand until the herb mix soaks into the buttermilk, at least 5 minutes. 5. Spray the top of the chicken with cooking spray. Bake for 10 minutes, then increase the temperature to 180°C and bake until an instant-read thermometer inserted into the thickest part of the breast reads 80°C and the chicken is deep golden brown, 30 to 35 minutes. 6. Transfer the chicken breast to a cutting board, let rest for 10 minutes, then cut the meat off the bone and cut into thick slices for serving.

Tex-Mex Turkey Burgers

Prep time: 10 minutes | Cook time: 14 to 16 minutes | Serves 4

30 g finely crushed corn tortilla chips	Pinch salt
1 egg, beaten	Freshly ground black pepper, to taste
60 g salsa	450 g turkey mince
70 g shredded pepper Jack cheese	1 tablespoon olive oil
	1 teaspoon paprika

1. Preheat the air fryer to 170ºC. 2. In a medium bowl, combine the tortilla chips, egg, salsa, cheese, salt, and pepper, and mix well. 3. Add the turkey and mix gently but thoroughly with clean hands. 4. Form the meat mixture into patties about ½ inch thick. Make an indentation in the centre of each patty with your thumb so the burgers don't puff up while cooking. 5. Brush the patties on both sides with the olive oil and sprinkle with paprika. 6. Put in the air fryer basket and air fry for 14 to 16 minutes or until the meat registers at least 76ºC. 7. Let sit for 5 minutes before serving.

Fajita Chicken Strips

Prep time: 10 minutes | Cook time: 15 minutes | Serves 4

450 g boneless, skinless chicken tenderloins, cut into strips	1 tablespoon olive oil
3 bell peppers, any color, cut into chunks	1 tablespoon fajita seasoning mix
1 onion, cut into chunks	Cooking spray

1. Preheat the air fryer to 190ºC. 2. In a large bowl, mix together the chicken, bell peppers, onion, olive oil, and fajita seasoning mix until completely coated. 3. Spray the air fryer basket lightly with cooking spray. 4. Place the chicken and vegetables in the air fryer basket and lightly spray with cooking spray. 5. Air fry for 7 minutes. Shake the basket and air fry for an additional 5 to 8 minutes, until the chicken is cooked through and the veggies are starting to char. 6. Serve warm.

Curried Orange Honey Chicken

Prep time: 10 minutes | Cook time: 16 to 19 minutes | Serves 4

340 g boneless, skinless chicken thighs, cut into 1-inch pieces	60 ml chicken stock
1 yellow bell pepper, cut into 1½-inch pieces	2 tablespoons honey
1 small red onion, sliced	60 ml orange juice
Olive oil for misting	1 tablespoon cornflour
	2 to 3 teaspoons curry powder

1. Preheat the air fryer to 190ºC. 2. Put the chicken thighs, pepper, and red onion in the air fryer basket and mist with olive oil. 3. Roast for 12 to 14 minutes or until the chicken is cooked to 76ºC, shaking the basket halfway through cooking time. 4. Remove the chicken and vegetables from the air fryer basket and set aside. 5. In a metal bowl, combine the stock, honey, orange juice, cornflour, and curry powder, and mix well. Add the chicken and vegetables, stir, and put the bowl in the basket. 6. Return the basket to the air fryer and roast for 2 minutes. Remove and stir, then roast for 2 to 3 minutes or until the sauce is thickened and bubbly. 7. Serve warm.

Chicken with Pineapple and Peach

Prep time: 10 minutes | Cook time: 14 to 15 minutes | Serves 4

1 450 g low-sodium boneless, skinless chicken breasts, cut into 1-inch pieces	safflower oil
1 medium red onion, chopped	1 peach, peeled, pitted, and cubed
1 (230 g) can pineapple chunks, drained, 60 ml juice reserved	1 tablespoon cornflour
1 tablespoon peanut oil or	½ teaspoon ground ginger
	¼ teaspoon ground allspice
	Brown rice, cooked (optional)

1. Preheat the air fryer to 196ºC. 2. In a medium metal bowl, mix the chicken, red onion, pineapple, and peanut oil. Bake in the air fryer for 9 minutes. Remove and stir. 3. Add the peach and return the bowl to the air fryer. Bake for 3 minutes more. Remove and stir again. 4. In a small bowl, whisk the reserved pineapple juice, the cornflour, ginger, and allspice well. Add to the chicken mixture and stir to combine. 5. Bake for 2 to 3 minutes more, or until the chicken reaches an internal temperature of 76ºC on a meat thermometer and the sauce is slightly thickened. 6. Serve immediately over hot cooked brown rice, if desired.

Tex-Mex Chicken Breasts

Prep time: 10 minutes | Cook time: 17 to 20 minutes | Serves 4

450 g low-sodium boneless, skinless chicken breasts, cut into 1-inch cubes	2 teaspoons olive oil
1 medium onion, chopped	115 g canned low-sodium black beans, rinsed and drained
1 red bell pepper, chopped	130 g low-sodium salsa
1 jalapeño pepper, minced	2 teaspoons chili powder

1. Preheat the air fryer to 200ºC. 2. In a medium metal bowl, mix the chicken, onion, bell pepper, jalapeño, and olive oil. Roast for 10 minutes, stirring once during cooking. 3. Add the black beans, salsa, and chili powder. Roast for 7 to 10 minutes more, stirring once, until the chicken reaches an internal temperature of 76ºC on a meat thermometer. Serve immediately.

Chicken Manchurian

450 g boneless, skinless chicken breasts, cut into 1-inch pieces

60 g ketchup

1 tablespoon tomato-based chili sauce, such as Heinz

1 tablespoon soy sauce

1 tablespoon rice vinegar

2 teaspoons vegetable oil

1 teaspoon hot sauce, such as Tabasco

½ teaspoon garlic powder

¼ teaspoon cayenne pepper

2 spring onions, thinly sliced

Cooked white rice, for serving

1. Preheat the air fryer to 180°C. 2. In a bowl, combine the chicken, ketchup, chili sauce, soy sauce, vinegar, oil, hot sauce, garlic powder, cayenne, and three-quarters of the spring onions and toss until evenly coated. 3. Scrape the chicken and sauce into a metal cake pan and place the pan in the air fryer. Bake until the chicken is cooked through and the sauce is reduced to a thick glaze, about 20 minutes, flipping the chicken pieces halfway through. 4. Remove the pan from the air fryer. Spoon the chicken and sauce over rice and top with the remaining spring onions. Serve immediately.

Chapter 4 Beef, Pork, and Lamb

Chapter 4 Beef, Pork, and Lamb

Chuck Kebab with Rocket

Prep time: 30 minutes | Cook time: 25 minutes | Serves 4

120 ml leeks, chopped
2 garlic cloves, smashed
900 g beef mince
Salt, to taste
¼ teaspoon ground black pepper, or more to taste
1 teaspoon cayenne pepper
½ teaspoon ground sumac
3 saffron threads
2 tablespoons loosely packed fresh flat-leaf parsley leaves
4 tablespoons tahini sauce
110 g baby rocket
1 tomato, cut into slices

1. In a bowl, mix the chopped leeks, garlic, beef mince, and spices; knead with your hands until everything is well incorporated. 2. Now, mound the beef mixture around a wooden skewer into a pointed-ended sausage. 3. Cook in the preheated air fryer at 182°C for 25 minutes. Serve your kebab with the tahini sauce, baby rocket and tomato. Enjoy!

Bacon-Wrapped Cheese Pork

Prep time: 10 minutes | Cook time: 20 minutes | Serves 4

4 (1-inch-thick) boneless pork chops
2 (150 g) packages Boursin
cheese
8 slices thin-cut bacon

1. Spray the air fryer basket with avocado oil. Preheat the air fryer to 204°C. 2. Place one of the chops on a cutting board. With a sharp knife held parallel to the cutting board, make a 1-inch-wide incision on the top edge of the chop. Carefully cut into the chop to form a large pocket, leaving a ½-inch border along the sides and bottom. Repeat with the other 3 chops. 3. Snip the corner of a large resealable plastic bag to form a ¾-inch hole. Place the Boursin cheese in the bag and pipe the cheese into the pockets in the chops, dividing the cheese evenly among them. 4. Wrap 2 slices of bacon around each chop and secure the ends with toothpicks. Place the bacon-wrapped chops in the air fryer basket and cook for 10 minutes, then flip the chops and cook for another 8 to 10 minutes, until the bacon is crisp, the chops are cooked through, and the internal temperature reaches 64°C. 5. Store leftovers in an airtight container in the refrigerator for up to 3 days. Reheat in a preheated 204°C air fryer for 5 minutes, or until warmed through.

Spicy Rump Steak

Prep time: 25 minutes | Cook time: 12 to 18 minutes | Serves 4

2 tablespoons salsa
1 tablespoon minced chipotle pepper or chipotle paste
1 tablespoon apple cider vinegar
1 teaspoon ground cumin
⅛ teaspoon freshly ground black
pepper
⅛ teaspoon red pepper flakes
340 g rump steak, cut into 4 pieces and gently pounded to about ⅓ inch thick
Cooking oil spray

1. In a small bowl, thoroughly mix the salsa, chipotle pepper, vinegar, cumin, black pepper, and red pepper flakes. Rub this mixture into both sides of each steak piece. Let stand for 15 minutes at room temperature. 2. Insert the crisper plate into the basket and place the basket into the unit. Preheat the unit by selecting AIR FRY, setting the temperature to 200°C, and setting the time to 3 minutes. Select START/STOP to begin. 3. Once the unit is preheated, spray the crisper plate with cooking oil. Working in batches, place 2 steaks into the basket. 4. Select AIR FRY, set the temperature to 200°C, and set the time to 9 minutes. Select START/STOP to begin. 5. After about 6 minutes, check the steaks. If a food thermometer inserted into the meat registers at least 64°C, they are done. If not, resume cooking. 6. When the cooking is done, transfer the steaks to a clean plate and cover with aluminum foil to keep warm. Repeat steps 3, 4, and 5 with the remaining steaks. 7. Thinly slice the steaks against the grain and serve.

Herb-Roasted Beef Tips with Onions

Prep time: 5 minutes | Cook time: 10 minutes | Serves 4

450 g rib eye steak, cubed
2 garlic cloves, minced
2 tablespoons olive oil
1 tablespoon fresh oregano
1 teaspoon salt
½ teaspoon black pepper
1 brown onion, thinly sliced

1. Preheat the air fryer to 192°C. 2. In a medium bowl, combine the steak, garlic, olive oil, oregano, salt, pepper, and onion. Mix until all of the beef and onion are well coated. 3. Put the seasoned steak mixture into the air fryer basket. Roast for 5 minutes. Stir and roast for 5 minutes more. 4. Let rest for 5 minutes before serving with some favorite sides.

Parmesan Herb Filet Mignon

Prep time: 20 minutes | Cook time: 13 minutes | Serves 4

450 g filet mignon

Sea salt and ground black pepper, to taste

½ teaspoon cayenne pepper

1 teaspoon dried basil

1 teaspoon dried rosemary

1 teaspoon dried thyme

1 tablespoon sesame oil

1 small-sized egg, well-whisked

120 ml Parmesan cheese, grated

1. Season the filet mignon with salt, black pepper, cayenne pepper, basil, rosemary, and thyme. Brush with sesame oil. 2. Put the egg in a shallow plate. Now, place the Parmesan cheese in another plate. 3. Coat the filet mignon with the egg; then lay it into the Parmesan cheese. Set the air fryer to 182°C. 4. Cook for 10 to 13 minutes or until golden. Serve with mixed salad leaves and enjoy!

Garlic Balsamic London Broil

Prep time: 30 minutes | Cook time: 8 to 10 minutes | Serves 8

900 g bavette or skirt steak

3 large garlic cloves, minced

3 tablespoons balsamic vinegar

3 tablespoons wholegrain mustard

2 tablespoons olive oil

Sea salt and ground black pepper, to taste

½ teaspoon dried hot red pepper flakes

1. Score both sides of the cleaned steak. 2. Thoroughly combine the remaining ingredients; massage this mixture into the meat to coat it on all sides. Let it marinate for at least 3 hours. 3. Set the air fryer to 204°C; Then cook the steak for 15 minutes. Flip it over and cook another 10 to 12 minutes. Bon appétit!

Beef Bavette Steak with Sage

Prep time: 13 minutes | Cook time: 7 minutes | Serves 2

80 ml sour cream

120 ml spring onion, chopped

1 tablespoon mayonnaise

3 cloves garlic, smashed

450 g beef bavette or skirt steak, trimmed and cubed

2 tablespoons fresh sage, minced

½ teaspoon salt

⅓ teaspoon black pepper, or to taste

1. Season your meat with salt and pepper; arrange beef cubes on the bottom of a baking dish that fits in your air fryer. 2. Stir in spring onions and garlic; air fry for about 7 minutes at 196°C. 3. Once your beef starts to tender, add the cream, mayonnaise, and sage; air fry an additional 8 minutes. Bon appétit!

Five-Spice Pork Belly

Prep time: 10 minutes | Cook time: 17 minutes | Serves 4

450 g unsalted pork belly

2 teaspoons Chinese five-spice powder

Sauce:

1 tablespoon coconut oil

1 (1-inch) piece fresh ginger, peeled and grated

2 cloves garlic, minced

120 ml beef or chicken stock

¼ to 120 ml liquid or powdered sweetener

3 tablespoons wheat-free tamari

1 spring onion, sliced, plus more for garnish

1. Spray the air fryer basket with avocado oil. Preheat the air fryer to 204°C. 2. Cut the pork belly into ½-inch-thick slices and season well on all sides with the five-spice powder. Place the slices in a single layer in the air fryer basket (if you're using a smaller air fryer, work in batches if necessary) and cook for 8 minutes, or until cooked to your liking, flipping halfway through. 3. While the pork belly cooks, make the sauce: Heat the coconut oil in a small saucepan over medium heat. Add the ginger and garlic and sauté for 1 minute, or until fragrant. Add the stock, sweetener, and tamari and simmer for 10 to 15 minutes, until thickened. Add the spring onion and cook for another minute, until the spring onion is softened. Taste and adjust the seasoning to your liking. 4. Transfer the pork belly to a large bowl. Pour the sauce over the pork belly and coat well. Place the pork belly slices on a serving platter and garnish with sliced spring onions. 5. Best served fresh. Store leftovers in an airtight container in the fridge for up to 4 days. Reheat in a preheated 204°C air fryer for 3 minutes, or until heated through.

Air Fryer Chicken-Fried Steak

Prep time: 5 minutes | Cook time: 20 minutes | Serves 4

450 g beef braising steak

700 ml low-fat milk, divided

1 teaspoon dried thyme

1 teaspoon dried rosemary

2 medium egg whites

235 ml gluten-free breadcrumbs

120 ml coconut flour

1 tablespoon Cajun seasoning

1. In a bowl, marinate the steak in 475 ml of milk for 30 to 45 minutes. 2. Remove the steak from milk, shake off the excess liquid, and season with the thyme and rosemary. Discard the milk. 3. In a shallow bowl, beat the egg whites with the remaining 235 ml of milk. 4. In a separate shallow bowl, combine the breadcrumbs, coconut flour, and seasoning. 5. Dip the steak in the egg white mixture then dredge in the breadcrumb mixture, coating well. 6. Place the steak in the basket of an air fryer. 7. Set the air fryer to 200°C, close, and cook for 10 minutes. 8. Open the air fryer, turn the steaks, close, and cook for 10 minutes. Let rest for 5 minutes.

Cheese Pork Chops

Prep time: 15 minutes | Cook time: 9 to 14 minutes | Serves 4

2 large eggs
120 ml finely grated Parmesan cheese
120 ml finely ground blanched almond flour or finely crushed pork scratchings
1 teaspoon paprika
½ teaspoon dried oregano
½ teaspoon garlic powder
Salt and freshly ground black pepper, to taste
570 g (1-inch-thick) boneless pork chops
Avocado oil spray

1. Beat the eggs in a shallow bowl. In a separate bowl, combine the Parmesan cheese, almond flour, paprika, oregano, garlic powder, and salt and pepper to taste. 2. Dip the pork chops into the eggs, then coat them with the Parmesan mixture, gently pressing the coating onto the meat. Spray the breaded pork chops with oil. 3. Set the air fryer to 204ºC. Place the pork chops in the air fryer basket in a single layer, working in batches if necessary. Cook for 6 minutes. Flip the chops and spray them with more oil. Cook for another 3 to 8 minutes, until an instant-read thermometer reads 64ºC. 4. Allow the pork chops to rest for at least 5 minutes, then serve.

Barbecue Ribs

Prep time: 5 minutes | Cook time: 30 minutes | Serves 4

1 (900 g) rack baby back ribs
1 teaspoon onion granules
1 teaspoon garlic powder
1 teaspoon light brown sugar
1 teaspoon dried oregano
Salt and freshly ground black pepper, to taste
Cooking oil spray
120 ml barbecue sauce

1. Use a sharp knife to remove the thin membrane from the back of the ribs. Cut the rack in half, or as needed, so the ribs fit in the air fryer basket. The best way to do this is to cut the ribs into 4- or 5-rib sections. 2. In a small bowl, stir together the onion granules, garlic powder, brown sugar, and oregano and season with salt and pepper. Rub the spice seasoning onto the front and back of the ribs. 3. Cover the ribs with plastic wrap or foil and let sit at room temperature for 30 minutes. 4. Insert the crisper plate into the basket and the basket into the unit. Preheat the unit by selecting AIR ROAST, setting the temperature to 182ºC, and setting the time to 3 minutes. Select START/STOP to begin. 5. Once the unit is preheated, spray the crisper plate with cooking oil. Place the ribs into the basket. It is okay to stack them. 6. Select AIR ROAST, set the temperature to 182ºC, and set the time to 30 minutes. Select START/STOP to begin. 7. After 15 minutes, flip the ribs. Resume cooking for 15 minutes, or until a food thermometer registers 88ºC. 8. When the cooking is complete, transfer the ribs to a serving dish. Drizzle the ribs with the barbecue sauce and serve.

Lamb and Cucumber Burgers

Prep time: 8 minutes | Cook time: 15 to 18 minutes | Serves 4

1 teaspoon ground ginger
½ teaspoon ground coriander
¼ teaspoon freshly ground white pepper
½ teaspoon ground cinnamon
½ teaspoon dried oregano
¼ teaspoon ground allspice
¼ teaspoon ground turmeric
120 ml low-fat plain Greek
yogurt
450 g lamb mince
1 teaspoon garlic paste
¼ teaspoon salt
¼ teaspoon freshly ground black pepper
Cooking oil spray
4 hamburger buns
½ cucumber, thinly sliced

1. In a small bowl, stir together the ginger, coriander, white pepper, cinnamon, oregano, allspice, and turmeric. 2. Put the yogurt in a small bowl and add half the spice mixture. Mix well and refrigerate. 3. Insert the crisper plate into the basket and the basket into the unit. Preheat the unit by selecting AIR FRY, setting the temperature to 182ºC, and setting the time to 3 minutes. Select START/STOP to begin. 4. In a large bowl, combine the lamb, garlic paste, remaining spice mix, salt, and pepper. Gently but thoroughly mix the ingredients with your hands. Form the meat into 4 patties. 5. Once the unit is preheated, spray the crisper plate with cooking oil, and place the patties into the basket. 6. Select AIR FRY, set the temperature to 182ºC, and set the time to 18 minutes. Select START/STOP to begin. 7. After 15 minutes, check the burgers. If a food thermometer inserted into the burgers registers 72ºC, the burgers are done. If not, resume cooking. 8. When the cooking is complete, assemble the burgers on the buns with cucumber slices and a dollop of the yogurt dip.

Super Bacon with Meat

Prep time: 5 minutes | Cook time: 1 hour | Serves 4

30 slices thick-cut bacon
110 g Cheddar cheese, shredded
340 g steak
280 g pork sausage meat
Salt and ground black pepper, to taste

1. Preheat the air fryer to 204ºC. 2. Lay out 30 slices of bacon in a woven pattern and bake for 20 minutes until crisp. Put the cheese in the center of the bacon. 3. Combine the steak and sausage to form a meaty mixture. 4. Lay out the meat in a rectangle of similar size to the bacon strips. Season with salt and pepper. 5. Roll the meat into a tight roll and refrigerate. 6. Preheat the air fryer to 204ºC. 7. Make a 7×7 bacon weave and roll the bacon weave over the meat, diagonally. 8. Bake for 60 minutes or until the internal temperature reaches at least 74ºC. 9. Let rest for 5 minutes before serving.

Panko Pork Chops

Prep time: 10 minutes | Cook time: 12 minutes | Serves 4

4 boneless pork chops, excess fat trimmed	1½ teaspoons paprika
¼ teaspoon salt	½ teaspoon granulated garlic
2 eggs	½ teaspoon onion granules
355 ml panko bread crumbs	1 teaspoon chili powder
3 tablespoons grated Parmesan cheese	¼ teaspoon freshly ground black pepper
	Olive oil spray

1. Sprinkle the pork chops with salt on both sides and let them sit while you prepare the seasonings and egg wash. 2. In a shallow medium bowl, beat the eggs. 3. In another shallow medium bowl, stir together the panko, Parmesan cheese, paprika, granulated garlic, onion granules, chili powder, and pepper. 4. Dip the pork chops in the egg and in the panko mixture to coat. Firmly press the crumbs onto the chops. 5. Insert the crisper plate into the basket and the basket into the unit. Preheat the unit by selecting AIR ROAST, setting the temperature to 204°C, and setting the time to 3 minutes. Select START/STOP to begin. 6. Once the unit is preheated, spray the crisper plate with olive oil. Place the pork chops into the basket and spray them with olive oil. 7. Select AIR ROAST, set the temperature to 204°C, and set the time to 12 minutes. Select START/STOP to begin. 8. After 6 minutes, flip the pork chops and spray them with more olive oil. Resume cooking. 9. When the cooking is complete, the chops should be golden and crispy and a food thermometer should register 64°C. Serve immediately.

Lebanese Malfouf (Stuffed Cabbage Rolls)

Prep time: 15 minutes | Cook time: 33 minutes | Serves 4

1 head green cabbage	2 tablespoons chopped fresh mint
450 g lean beef mince	Juice of 1 lemon
120 ml long-grain brown rice	Olive oil cooking spray
4 garlic cloves, minced	120 ml beef stock
1 teaspoon salt	1 tablespoon olive oil
½ teaspoon black pepper	
1 teaspoon ground cinnamon	

1. Cut the cabbage in half and remove the core. Remove 12 of the larger leaves to use for the cabbage rolls. 2. Bring a large pot of salted water to a boil, then drop the cabbage leaves into the water, boiling them for 3 minutes. Remove from the water and set aside. 3. In a large bowl, combine the beef, rice, garlic, salt, pepper, cinnamon, mint, and lemon juice, and mix together until combined. Divide this mixture into 12 equal portions. 4. Preheat the air fryer to 182°C. Lightly coat a small casserole dish with olive oil cooking spray. 5. Place a cabbage leaf on a clean work surface. Place a spoonful of the beef mixture on one side of the leaf, leaving space on all other sides. Fold the two perpendicular sides inward and then roll forward, tucking tightly as rolled (similar to a burrito roll). Place the finished rolls into the baking dish, stacking them on top of each other if needed. 6. Pour the beef stock over the top of the cabbage rolls so that it soaks down between them, and then brush the tops with the olive oil. 7. Place the casserole dish into the air fryer basket and bake for 30 minutes.

Italian Sausage Links

Prep time: 10 minutes | Cook time: 24 minutes | Serves 4

1 pepper (any color), sliced	Sea salt and freshly ground black pepper, to taste
1 medium onion, sliced	450 g Italian-seasoned sausage links
1 tablespoon avocado oil	
1 teaspoon Italian seasoning	

1. Place the pepper and onion in a medium bowl, and toss with the avocado oil, Italian seasoning, and salt and pepper to taste. 2. Set the air fryer to 204°C. Put the vegetables in the air fryer basket and cook for 12 minutes. 3. Push the vegetables to the side of the basket and arrange the sausage links in the bottom of the basket in a single layer. Spoon the vegetables over the sausages. Cook for 12 minutes, tossing halfway through, until an instant-read thermometer inserted into the sausage reads 72°C.

Greek Pork with Tzatziki Sauce

Prep time: 30 minutes | Cook time: 50 minutes | Serves 4

Greek Pork:	2 cloves garlic, finely chopped
900 g pork loin roasting joint	Tzatziki:
Salt and black pepper, to taste	½ cucumber, finely chopped and squeezed
1 teaspoon smoked paprika	235 ml full-fat Greek yogurt
½ teaspoon mustard seeds	1 garlic clove, minced
½ teaspoon celery salt	1 tablespoon extra-virgin olive oil
1 teaspoon fennel seeds	1 teaspoon balsamic vinegar
1 teaspoon chili powder	1 teaspoon minced fresh dill
1 teaspoon turmeric powder	A pinch of salt
½ teaspoon ground ginger	
2 tablespoons olive oil	

1. Toss all ingredients for Greek pork in a large mixing bowl. Toss until the meat is well coated. 2. Cook in the preheated air fryer at 182°C for 30 minutes; turn over and cook another 20 minutes. 3. Meanwhile, prepare the tzatziki by mixing all the tzatziki ingredients. Place in your refrigerator until ready to use. 4. Serve the pork sirloin roast with the chilled tzatziki on the side. Enjoy!

Beef and Goat Cheese Stuffed Peppers

Prep time: 10 minutes | Cook time: 30 minutes | Serves 4

450 g lean beef mince
120 ml cooked brown rice
2 plum tomatoes, diced
3 garlic cloves, minced
½ brown onion, diced
2 tablespoons fresh oregano, chopped

1 teaspoon salt
½ teaspoon black pepper
¼ teaspoon ground allspice
2 peppers, halved and seeded
110 g goat cheese
60 ml fresh parsley, chopped

1. Preheat the air fryer to 182°C. 2. In a large bowl, combine the beef, rice, tomatoes, garlic, onion, oregano, salt, pepper, and allspice. Mix well. 3. Divide the beef mixture equally into the halved peppers and top each with about a quarter of the goat cheese. 4. Place the peppers into the air fryer basket in a single layer, making sure that they don't touch each other. Bake for 30 minutes. 5. Remove the peppers from the air fryer and top with fresh parsley before serving.

Steak, Broccoli, and Mushroom Rice Bowls

Prep time: 10 minutes | Cook time: 15 to 18 minutes | Serves 4

2 tablespoons cornflour
120 ml low-sodium beef stock
1 teaspoon reduced-salt soy sauce
340 g rump steak, cut into 1-inch cubes
120 ml broccoli florets

1 onion, chopped
235 ml sliced white or chestnut mushrooms
1 tablespoon grated peeled fresh ginger
Cooked brown rice (optional), for serving

1. In a medium bowl, stir together the cornflour, beef stock, and soy sauce until the cornflour is completely dissolved. 2. Add the beef cubes and toss to coat. Let stand for 5 minutes at room temperature. 3. Insert the crisper plate into the basket and the basket into the unit. Preheat the unit by selecting AIR FRY, setting the temperature to 204°C, and setting the time to 3 minutes. Select START/STOP to begin. 4. Once the unit is preheated, use a slotted spoon to transfer the beef from the stock mixture into a medium metal bowl that fits into the basket. Reserve the stock. Add the broccoli, onion, mushrooms, and ginger to the beef. Place the bowl into the basket. 5. Select AIR FRY, set the temperature to 204°C, and set the time to 18 minutes. Select START/STOP to begin. 6. After about 12 minutes, check the beef and broccoli. If a food thermometer inserted into the beef registers at least 64°C and the vegetables are tender, add the reserved stock and resume cooking for about 3 minutes until the sauce boils. If not, resume cooking for about 3 minutes before adding the reservedstock. 7. When the cooking is complete, serve immediately over hot cooked brown rice, if desired.

Spicy Tomato Beef Meatballs

Prep time: 10 minutes | Cook time: 15 minutes | Serves 4

3 spring onions, minced
1 garlic clove, minced
1 egg yolk
60 ml cream cracker crumbs
Pinch salt
Freshly ground black pepper, to

taste
450 g 95% lean beef mince
Olive oil spray
300 ml any tomato pasta sauce
2 tablespoons Dijon mustard

1. In a large bowl, combine the spring onionspring onions, garlic, egg yolk, cracker crumbs, salt, and pepper and mix well. 2. Add the beef and gently but thoroughly mix with your hands until combined. Form the meat mixture into 1½-inch round meatballs. 3. Insert the crisper plate into the basket and the basket into the unit. Preheat the unit by selecting BAKE, setting the temperature to 204°C, and setting the time to 3 minutes. Select START/STOP to begin. 4. Once the unit is preheated, spray the crisper plate with olive oil. Working in batches, spray the meatballs with olive oil and place them into the basket in a single layer, without touching. 5. Select BAKE, set the temperature to 204°C, and set the time to 11 minutes. Select START/STOP to begin. 6. When the cooking is complete, a food thermometer inserted into the meatballs should register 74°C. Transfer the meatballs to a 6-inch metal bowl. 7. Repeat steps 4, 5, and 6 with the remaining meatballs. 8. Top the meatballs with the pasta sauce and Dijon mustard, and mix gently. Place the bowl into the basket. 9. Select BAKE, set the temperature to 204°C, and set the time to 4 minutes. Select START/STOP to begin. 10. When the cooking is complete, serve hot.

Greek-Style Meatloaf

Prep time: 5 minutes | Cook time: 25 minutes | Serves 6

450 g lean beef mince
2 eggs
2 plum tomatoes, diced
½ brown onion, diced
120 ml whole wheat bread crumbs
1 teaspoon garlic powder
1 teaspoon dried oregano

1 teaspoon dried thyme
1 teaspoon salt
1 teaspoon black pepper
60 g mozzarella cheese, shredded
1 tablespoon olive oil
Fresh chopped parsley, for garnish

1. Preheat the oven to 192°C. 2. In a large bowl, mix together the beef, eggs, tomatoes, onion, bread crumbs, garlic powder, oregano, thyme, salt, pepper, and cheese. 3. Form into a loaf, flattening to 1-inch thick. 4. Brush the top with olive oil, then place the meatloaf into the air fryer basket and cook for 25 minutes. 5. Remove from the air fryer and allow to rest for 5 minutes, before slicing and serving with a sprinkle of parsley.

Onion Pork Kebabs

Prep time: 22 minutes | Cook time: 18 minutes | Serves 3

2 tablespoons tomato purée
½ fresh green chilli, minced
⅓ teaspoon paprika
450 g pork mince
120 ml spring onions, finely chopped

3 cloves garlic, peeled and finely minced
1 teaspoon ground black pepper, or more to taste
1 teaspoon salt, or more to taste

1. Thoroughly combine all ingredients in a mixing dish. Then form your mixture into sausage shapes. 2. Cook for 18 minutes at 179ºC. Mound salad on a serving platter, top with air-fried kebabs and serve warm. Bon appétit!

Pork Loin Roast

Prep time: 30 minutes | Cook time: 55 minutes | Serves 6

680 g boneless pork loin joint, washed
1 teaspoon mustard seeds
1 teaspoon garlic powder
1 teaspoon porcini powder
1 teaspoon onion granules

¾ teaspoon sea salt flakes
1 teaspoon red pepper flakes, crushed
2 dried sprigs thyme, crushed
2 tablespoons lime juice

1. Firstly, score the meat using a small knife; make sure to not cut too deep. 2. In a small-sized mixing dish, combine all seasonings in the order listed above; mix to combine well. 3. Massage the spice mix into the pork meat to evenly distribute. Drizzle with lemon juice. 4. Set the air fryer to 182ºC. Place the pork in the air fryer basket; roast for 25 to 30 minutes. Pause the machine, check for doneness and cook for 25 minutes more.

Saucy Beef Fingers

Prep time: 30 minutes | Cook time: 14 minutes | Serves 4

680 g rump steak
60 ml red wine
60 ml fresh lime juice
1 teaspoon garlic powder
1 teaspoon onion granules
1 teaspoon celery salt
1 teaspoon mustard seeds

Coarse sea salt and ground black pepper, to taste
1 teaspoon red pepper flakes
2 eggs, lightly whisked
235 ml Parmesan cheese
1 teaspoon paprika

1. Place the steak, red wine, lime juice, garlic powder, onion granules, celery salt, mustard seeds, salt, black pepper, and red pepper in a large ceramic bowl; let it marinate for 3 hours. 2.

Tenderize the steak by pounding with a mallet; cut into 1-inch strips. 3. In a shallow bowl, whisk the eggs. In another bowl, mix the Parmesan cheese and paprika. 4. Dip the beef pieces into the whisked eggs and coat on all sides. Now, dredge the beef pieces in the Parmesan mixture. 5. Cook at 204ºC for 14 minutes, flipping halfway through the cooking time. 6. Meanwhile, make the sauce by heating the reserved marinade in a saucepan over medium heat; let it simmer until thoroughly warmed. Serve the steak fingers with the sauce on the side. Enjoy!

Lemon Pork with Marjoram

Prep time: 5 minutes | Cook time: 10 minutes | Serves 4

1 (450 g) pork tenderloin, cut into ½-inch-thick slices
1 tablespoon extra-virgin olive oil
1 tablespoon freshly squeezed lemon juice
1 tablespoon honey

½ teaspoon grated lemon zest
½ teaspoon dried marjoram leaves
Pinch salt
Freshly ground black pepper, to taste
Cooking oil spray

1. Put the pork slices in a medium bowl. 2. In a small bowl, whisk the olive oil, lemon juice, honey, lemon zest, marjoram, salt, and pepper until combined. Pour this marinade over the tenderloin slices and gently massage with your hands to work it into the pork. 3. Insert the crisper plate into the basket and the basket into the unit. Preheat the unit by selecting AIR ROAST, setting the temperature to 204ºC, and setting the time to 3 minutes. Select START/STOP to begin. 4. Once the unit is preheated, spray the crisper plate with cooking oil. Place the pork into the basket. 5. Select AIR ROAST, set the temperature to 204ºC, and set the time to 10 minutes. Select START/STOP to begin. 6. When the cooking is complete, a food thermometer inserted into the pork should register at least 64ºC. Let the pork stand for 5 minutes and serve.

BBQ Pork Steaks

Prep time: 5 minutes | Cook time: 15 minutes | Serves 4

4 pork steaks
1 tablespoon Cajun seasoning
2 tablespoons BBQ sauce
1 tablespoon vinegar

1 teaspoon soy sauce
120 ml brown sugar
120 ml ketchup

1. Preheat the air fryer to 143ºC. 2. Sprinkle pork steaks with Cajun seasoning. 3. Combine remaining ingredients and brush onto steaks. 4. Add coated steaks to air fryer. Air fry 15 minutes until just browned. 5. Serve immediately.

Broccoli and Pork Teriyaki

Prep time: 10 minutes | Cook time: 13 minutes | Serves 4

1 head broccoli, trimmed into florets

1 tablespoon extra-virgin olive oil

¼ teaspoon sea salt

¼ teaspoon freshly ground black pepper

450 g pork tenderloin, trimmed and cut into 1-inch pieces

120 ml teriyaki sauce, divided

Olive oil spray

475 ml cooked brown rice

Sesame seeds, for garnish

1. Insert the crisper plate into the basket and the basket into the unit. Preheat the unit by selecting AIR ROAST, setting the temperature to 204°C, and setting the time to 3 minutes. Select START/STOP to begin. 2. In a large bowl, toss together the broccoli, olive oil, salt, and pepper. 3. In a medium bowl, toss together the pork and 3 tablespoons of teriyaki sauce to coat the meat. 4. Once the unit is preheated, spray the crisper plate with olive oil. Put the broccoli and pork into the basket. Spray them with olive oil and drizzle with 1 tablespoon of teriyaki sauce. 5. Select AIR ROAST, set the temperature to 204°C, and set the time to 13 minutes. Select START/STOP to begin. 6. After 10 to 12 minutes, the broccoli is tender and light golden brown and a food thermometer inserted into the pork should register 64°C. Remove the basket and drizzle the broccoli and pork with the remaining 60 ml of teriyaki sauce and toss to coat. Reinsert the basket to resume cooking for 1 minute. 7. When the cooking is complete, serve immediately over the hot cooked rice, if desired, garnished with the sesame seeds.

Pork Medallions with Endive Salad

Prep time: 25 minutes | Cook time: 7 minutes | Serves 4

1 (230 g) pork tenderloin

Salt and freshly ground black pepper, to taste

60 ml flour

2 eggs, lightly beaten

180 ml finely crushed crackers

1 teaspoon paprika

1 teaspoon mustard powder

1 teaspoon garlic powder

1 teaspoon dried thyme

1 teaspoon salt

vegetable or rapeseed oil, in spray bottle

Vinaigrette:

60 ml white balsamic vinegar

2 tablespoons agave syrup (or

honey or maple syrup)

1 tablespoon Dijon mustard

juice of ½ lemon

2 tablespoons chopped chervil or flat-leaf parsley

salt and freshly ground black pepper

120 ml extra-virgin olive oil

Endive Salad:

1 heart romaine lettuce, torn into large pieces

2 heads endive, sliced

120 ml cherry tomatoes, halved

85 g fresh Mozzarella, diced

Salt and freshly ground black pepper, to taste

1. Slice the pork tenderloin into 1-inch slices. Using a meat pounder, pound the pork slices into thin ½-inch medallions. Generously season the pork with salt and freshly ground black pepper on both sides. 2. Set up a dredging station using three shallow dishes. Put the flour in one dish and the beaten eggs in a second dish. Combine the crushed crackers, paprika, mustard powder, garlic powder, thyme and salt in a third dish. 3. Preheat the air fryer to 204°C. 4. Dredge the pork medallions in flour first and then into the beaten egg. Let the excess egg drip off and coat both sides of the medallions with the cracker crumb mixture. Spray both sides of the coated medallions with vegetable or rapeseed oil. 5. Air fry the medallions in two batches at 204°C for 5 minutes. Once you have air-fried all the medallions, flip them all over and return the first batch of medallions back into the air fryer on top of the second batch. Air fry at 204°C for an additional 2 minutes. 6. While the medallions are cooking, make the salad and dressing. Whisk the white balsamic vinegar, agave syrup, Dijon mustard, lemon juice, chervil, salt and pepper together in a small bowl. Whisk in the olive oil slowly until combined and thickened. 7. Combine the romaine lettuce, endive, cherry tomatoes, and Mozzarella cheese in a large salad bowl. Drizzle the dressing over the vegetables and toss to combine. Season with salt and freshly ground black pepper. 8. Serve the pork medallions warm on or beside the salad.

Cheese Wine Pork Loin

Prep time: 30 minutes | Cook time: 15 minutes | Serves 2

235 ml water

235 ml red wine

1 tablespoon sea salt

2 pork loin steaks

60 ml ground almonds

60 ml flaxseed meal

½ teaspoon baking powder

1 teaspoon onion granules

½ teaspoon porcini powder

Sea salt and ground black pepper, to taste

1 egg

60 ml yoghurt

1 teaspoon wholegrain or English mustard

80 ml Parmesan cheese, grated

1. In a large ceramic dish, combine the water, wine and salt. Add the pork and put for 1 hour in the refrigerator. 2. In a shallow bowl, mix the ground almonds, flaxseed meal, baking powder, onion granules, porcini powder, salt, and ground pepper. In another bowl, whisk the eggs with yoghurt and mustard. 3. In a third bowl, place the grated Parmesan cheese. 4. Dip the pork in the seasoned flour mixture and toss evenly; then, in the egg mixture. Finally, roll them over the grated Parmesan cheese. 5. Spritz the bottom of the air fryer basket with cooking oil. Add the breaded pork and cook at 202°C and for 10 minutes. 6. Flip and cook for 5 minutes more on the other side. Serve warm.

Kale and Beef Omelet

Prep time: 15 minutes | Cook time: 16 minutes | Serves 4

230 g leftover beef, coarsely chopped	4 eggs, beaten
2 garlic cloves, pressed	4 tablespoons double cream
235 ml kale, torn into pieces and wilted	½ teaspoon turmeric powder
1 tomato, chopped	Salt and ground black pepper, to taste
¼ teaspoon sugar	⅛ teaspoon ground allspice
	Cooking spray

1. Preheat the air fryer to 182ºC. Spritz four ramekins with cooking spray. 2. Put equal amounts of each of the ingredients into each ramekin and mix well. 3. Air fry for 16 minutes. Serve immediately.

Italian Pork Loin

Prep time: 30 minutes | Cook time: 16 minutes | Serves 3

1 teaspoon sea salt	2 garlic cloves, minced
½ teaspoon black pepper, freshly cracked	450 g pork loin joint
60 ml red wine	1 tablespoon Italian herb seasoning blend
2 tablespoons mustard	

1. In a ceramic bowl, mix the salt, black pepper, red wine, mustard, and garlic. Add the pork loin and let it marinate at least 30 minutes. 2. Spritz the sides and bottom of the air fryer basket with nonstick cooking spray. 3. Place the pork loin in the basket; sprinkle with the Italian herb seasoning blend. Cook the pork loin at 188ºC for 10 minutes. Flip halfway through, spraying with cooking oil and cook for 5 to 6 minutes more. Serve immediately.

Bacon Wrapped Pork with Apple Gravy

Prep time: 10 minutes | Cook time: 25 minutes | Serves 4

Pork:	1 small shallot, chopped
1 tablespoons Dijon mustard	2 apples
1 pork tenderloin	1 tablespoon almond flour
3 strips bacon	235 ml vegetable stock
Apple Gravy:	½ teaspoon Dijon mustard
3 tablespoons ghee, divided	

1. Preheat the air fryer to 182ºC. 2. Spread Dijon mustard all over tenderloin and wrap with strips of bacon. 3. Put into air fryer and air fry for 12 minutes. Use a meat thermometer to check for doneness. 4. To make sauce, heat 1 tablespoons of ghee in a pan and add shallots. Cook for 1 minute. 5. Then add apples, cooking for 4 minutes until softened. 6. Add flour and 2 tablespoons of ghee to make a roux. Add stock and mustard, stirring well to combine. 7. When sauce starts to bubble, add 235 ml of sautéed apples, cooking until sauce thickens. 8. Once pork tenderloin is cooked, allow to sit 8 minutes to rest before slicing. 9. Serve topped with apple gravy.

Beef and Spinach Rolls

Prep time: 10 minutes | Cook time: 14 minutes | Serves 2

3 teaspoons pesto	85 g roasted red peppers
900 g beef bavette or skirt steak	180 ml baby spinach
6 slices low-moisture Mozarella or other melting cheese	1 teaspoon sea salt
	1 teaspoon black pepper

1. Preheat the air fryer to 204ºC. 2. Spoon equal amounts of the pesto onto each steak and spread it across evenly. 3. Put the cheese, roasted red peppers and spinach on top of the meat, about three-quarters of the way down. 4. Roll the steak up, holding it in place with toothpicks. Sprinkle with the sea salt and pepper. 5. Put inside the air fryer and air fry for 14 minutes, turning halfway through the cooking time. 6. Allow the beef to rest for 10 minutes before slicing up and serving.

Pork Kebab with Yogurt Sauce

Prep time: 25 minutes | Cook time: 12 minutes | Serves 4

2 teaspoons olive oil	½ teaspoon celery salt
230 g pork mince	Yogurt Sauce:
230 g beef mince	2 tablespoons olive oil
1 egg, whisked	2 tablespoons fresh lemon juice
Sea salt and ground black pepper, to taste	Sea salt, to taste
1 teaspoon paprika	¼ teaspoon red pepper flakes, crushed
2 garlic cloves, minced	120 ml full-fat yogurt
1 teaspoon dried marjoram	1 teaspoon dried dill
1 teaspoon mustard seeds	

1. Spritz the sides and bottom of the air fryer basket with 2 teaspoons of olive oil. 2. In a mixing dish, thoroughly combine the pork, beef, egg, salt, black pepper, paprika, garlic, marjoram, mustard seeds, and celery salt. 3. Form the mixture into kebabs and transfer them to the greased basket. Cook at 185ºC for 11 to 12 minutes, turning them over once or twice. In the meantime, mix all the sauce ingredients and place in the refrigerator until ready to serve. Serve the pork kebabs with the yogurt sauce on the side. Enjoy!

Herbed Beef

Prep time: 5 minutes | Cook time: 22 minutes | Serves 6

1 teaspoon dried dill

1 teaspoon dried thyme

1 teaspoon garlic powder

900 g beef steak

3 tablespoons butter

1. Preheat the air fryer to 182ºC. 2. Combine the dill, thyme, and garlic powder in a small bowl, and massage into the steak. 3. Air fry the steak in the air fryer for 20 minutes, then remove, shred, and return to the air fryer. 4. Add the butter and air fry the shredded steak for a further 2 minutes at 185ºC. Make sure the beef is coated in the butter before serving.

Beef and Pork Sausage Meatloaf

Prep time: 20 minutes | Cook time: 25 minutes | Serves 4

340 g beef mince

110 g pork sausage meat

235 ml shallots, finely chopped

2 eggs, well beaten

3 tablespoons milk

1 tablespoon oyster sauce

1 teaspoon porcini mushrooms

½ teaspoon cumin powder

1 teaspoon garlic paste

1 tablespoon fresh parsley

Salt and crushed red pepper flakes, to taste

235 ml crushed cream crackers

Cooking spray

1. Preheat the air fryer to 182ºC. Spritz a baking dish with cooking spray. 2. Mix all the ingredients in a large bowl, combining everything well. 3. Transfer to the baking dish and bake in the air fryer for 25 minutes. 4. Serve hot.

Greek Lamb Rack

Prep time: 5 minutes | Cook time: 10 minutes | Serves 4

60 ml freshly squeezed lemon juice

1 teaspoon oregano

2 teaspoons minced fresh rosemary

1 teaspoon minced fresh thyme

2 tablespoons minced garlic

Salt and freshly ground black pepper, to taste

2 to 4 tablespoons olive oil

1 lamb rib rack (7 to 8 ribs)

1. Preheat the air fryer to 182ºC. 2. In a small mixing bowl, combine the lemon juice, oregano, rosemary, thyme, garlic, salt, pepper, and olive oil and mix well. 3. Rub the mixture over the lamb, covering all the meat. Put the rack of lamb in the air fryer. Roast for 10 minutes. Flip the rack halfway through. 4. After 10 minutes, measure the internal temperature of the rack of lamb reaches at least 64ºC. 5. Serve immediately.

Cheddar Bacon Burst with Spinach

Prep time: 5 minutes | Cook time: 60 minutes | Serves 8

30 slices bacon

1 tablespoon Chipotle chilli powder

2 teaspoons Italian seasoning

120 ml Cheddar cheese

1 L raw spinach

1. Preheat the air fryer to 192ºC. 2. Weave the bacon into 15 vertical pieces and 12 horizontal pieces. Cut the extra 3 in half to fill in the rest, horizontally. 3. Season the bacon with Chipotle chilli powder and Italian seasoning. 4. Add the cheese to the bacon. 5. Add the spinach and press down to compress. 6. Tightly roll up the woven bacon. 7. Line a baking sheet with kitchen foil and add plenty of salt to it. 8. Put the bacon on top of a cooling rack and put that on top of the baking sheet. 9. Bake for 60 minutes. 10. Let cool for 15 minutes before slicing and serving.

Beef Fillet with Thyme and Parsley

Prep time: 5 minutes | Cook time: 15 minutes | Serves 4

1 tablespoon butter, melted

¼ dried thyme

1 teaspoon garlic salt

¼ teaspoon dried parsley

450 g beef fillet

1. Preheat the air fryer to 204ºC. 2. In a bowl, combine the melted butter, thyme, garlic salt, and parsley. 3. Cut the beef fillet into slices and generously apply the seasoned butter using a brush. Transfer to the air fryer basket. 4. Air fry the beef for 15 minutes. 5. Take care when removing it and serve hot.

Italian Lamb Chops with Avocado Mayo

Prep time: 5 minutes | Cook time: 12 minutes | Serves 2

2 lamp chops

2 teaspoons Italian herbs

2 avocados

120 ml mayonnaise

1 tablespoon lemon juice

1. Season the lamb chops with the Italian herbs, then set aside for 5 minutes. 2. Preheat the air fryer to 204ºC and place the rack inside. 3. Put the chops on the rack and air fry for 12 minutes. 4. In the meantime, halve the avocados and open to remove the pits. Spoon the flesh into a blender. 5. Add the mayonnaise and lemon juice and pulse until a smooth consistency is achieved. 6. Take care when removing the chops from the air fryer, then plate up and serve with the avocado mayo.

Greek Lamb Pitta Pockets

Prep time: 15 minutes | Cook time: 6 minutes | Serves 4

Dressing:

235 ml plain yogurt

1 tablespoon lemon juice

1 teaspoon dried dill, crushed

1 teaspoon ground oregano

½ teaspoon salt

Meatballs:

230 g lamb mince

1 tablespoon diced onion

1 teaspoon dried parsley

1 teaspoon dried dill, crushed

¼ teaspoon oregano

¼ teaspoon coriander

¼ teaspoon ground cumin

¼ teaspoon salt

4 pitta halves

Suggested Toppings:

1 red onion, slivered

1 medium cucumber, deseeded, thinly sliced

Crumbled feta cheese

Sliced black olives

Chopped fresh peppers

1. Preheat the air fryer to 200°C. 2. Stir the dressing ingredients together in a small bowl and refrigerate while preparing lamb. 3. Combine all meatball ingredients in a large bowl and stir to distribute seasonings. 4. Shape meat mixture into 12 small meatballs, rounded or slightly flattened if you prefer. 5. Transfer the meatballs in the preheated air fryer and air fry for 6 minutes, until well done. Remove and drain on paper towels. 6. To serve, pile meatballs and the choice of toppings in pitta pockets and drizzle with dressing.

Spinach and Beef Braciole

Prep time: 25 minutes | Cook time: 1 hour 32 minutes | Serves 4

½ onion, finely chopped

1 teaspoon olive oil

80 ml red wine

475 ml crushed tomatoes

1 teaspoon Italian seasoning

½ teaspoon garlic powder

¼ teaspoon crushed red pepper flakes

2 tablespoons chopped fresh parsley

2 bavette or skirt steaks (about 680 g)

salt and freshly ground black pepper

475 ml fresh spinach, chopped

1 clove minced garlic

120 ml roasted red peppers, julienned

120 ml grated pecorino cheese

60 ml pine nuts, toasted and roughly chopped

2 tablespoons olive oil

1. Preheat the air fryer to 204°C. 2. Toss the onions and olive oil together in a baking pan or casserole dish. Air fry at 204°C for 5 minutes, stirring a couple times during the cooking process. Add the red wine, crushed tomatoes, Italian seasoning, garlic powder, red pepper flakes and parsley and stir. Cover the pan tightly with aluminum foil, lower the air fryer temperature to 176°C and continue to air fry for 15 minutes. 3. While the sauce is simmering, prepare the beef. Using a meat mallet, pound the beef until it is ¼-inch thick. Season both sides of the beef with salt and pepper. Combine the spinach, garlic, red peppers, pecorino cheese, pine nuts and olive oil in a medium bowl. Season with salt and freshly ground black pepper. Disperse the mixture over the steaks. Starting at one of the short ends, roll the beef around the filling, tucking in the sides as you roll to ensure the filling is completely enclosed. Secure the beef rolls with toothpicks. 4. Remove the baking pan with the sauce from the air fryer and set it aside. Preheat the air fryer to 204°C. 5. Brush or spray the beef rolls with a little olive oil and air fry at 204°C for 12 minutes, rotating the beef during the cooking process for even browning. When the beef is browned, submerge the rolls into the sauce in the baking pan, cover the pan with foil and return it to the air fryer. Reduce the temperature of the air fryer to 121°C and air fry for 60 minutes. 6. Remove the beef rolls from the sauce. Cut each roll into slices and serve, ladling some sauce overtop.

Chapter 5 Fish and Seafood

Chapter 5 Fish and Seafood

Honey-Glazed Salmon

Prep time: 5 minutes | Cook time: 12 minutes | Serves 4

60 ml raw honey	½ teaspoon salt
4 garlic cloves, minced	Olive oil cooking spray
1 tablespoon olive oil	4 (1½-inch-thick) salmon fillets

1. Preheat the air fryer to 192ºC. 2. In a small bowl, mix together the honey, garlic, olive oil, and salt. 3. Spray the bottom of the air fryer basket with olive oil cooking spray, and place the salmon in a single layer on the bottom of the air fryer basket. 4. Brush the top of each fillet with the honey-garlic mixture, and roast for 10 to 12 minutes, or until the internal temperature reaches 64ºC.

Tilapia Sandwiches with Tartar Sauce

Prep time: 8 minutes | Cook time: 17 minutes | Serves 4

160 g mayonnaise	40 g plain flour
2 tablespoons dried minced onion	1 egg, lightly beaten
1 dill pickle spear, finely chopped	200 g panko bread crumbs
2 teaspoons pickle juice	2 teaspoons lemon pepper
¼ teaspoon salt	4 x 170 g tilapia fillets
⅛ teaspoon freshly ground black pepper	Olive oil spray
	4 soft sub rolls
	4 lettuce leaves

1. To make the tartar sauce, in a small bowl, whisk the mayonnaise, dried onion, pickle, pickle juice, salt, and pepper until blended. Refrigerate while you make the fish. 2. Scoop the flour onto a plate; set aside. 3. Put the beaten egg in a medium shallow bowl. 4. On another plate, stir together the panko and lemon pepper. 5. Insert the crisper plate into the basket and the basket into the unit. Preheat the unit to 204ºC. 6. Dredge the tilapia fillets in the flour, in the egg, and press into the panko mixture to coat. 7. Once the unit is preheated, spray the crisper plate with olive oil and place a baking paper liner into the basket. Place the prepared fillets on the liner in a single layer. Lightly spray the fillets with olive oil. 8. cook for 8 minutes, remove the basket, carefully flip the fillets, and spray them with more olive oil. Reinsert the basket to resume cooking. 9. When the cooking is complete, the fillets should be golden and crispy and a food thermometer should register 64ºC. Place each cooked fillet in a sub roll, top with a little bit of tartar sauce and lettuce, and serve.

Salmon Burgers with Creamy Broccoli Slaw

Prep time: 15 minutes | Cook time: 10 minutes | Serves 4

For the salmon burgers	For the broccoli slaw
455 g salmon fillets, bones and skin removed	270 g chopped or shredded broccoli
1 egg	25 g shredded carrots
10 g fresh dill, chopped	30 g sunflower seeds
60 g fresh whole wheat bread crumbs	2 garlic cloves, minced
½ teaspoon salt	½ teaspoon salt
½ teaspoon cayenne pepper	2 tablespoons apple cider vinegar
2 garlic cloves, minced	285 g nonfat plain Greek yogurt
4 whole wheat buns	

Make the salmon burgers 1. Preheat the air fryer to 182ºC. 2. In a food processor, pulse the salmon fillets until they are finely chopped. 3. In a large bowl, combine the chopped salmon, egg, dill, bread crumbs, salt, cayenne, and garlic until it comes together. 4. Form the salmon into 4 patties. Place them into the air fryer basket, making sure that they don't touch each other. 5. Bake for 5 minutes. Flip the salmon patties and bake for 5 minutes more. Make the broccoli slaw 6. In a large bowl, combine all of the ingredients for the broccoli slaw. Mix well. 7. Serve the salmon burgers on toasted whole wheat buns, and top with a generous portion of broccoli slaw.

Baked Grouper with Tomatoes and Garlic

Prep time: 5 minutes | Cook time: 12 minutes | Serves 4

4 grouper fillets	45 g sliced Kalamata olives
½ teaspoon salt	10 g fresh dill, roughly chopped
3 garlic cloves, minced	Juice of 1 lemon
1 tomato, sliced	¼ cup olive oil

1. Preheat the air fryer to 192ºC. 2. Season the grouper fillets on all sides with salt, then place into the air fryer basket and top with the minced garlic, tomato slices, olives, and fresh dill. 3. Drizzle the lemon juice and olive oil over the top of the grouper, then bake for 10 to 12 minutes, or until the internal temperature reaches 64ºC.

Prawns Pasta with Basil and Mushrooms

Prep time: 10 minutes | Cook time: 10 minutes | Serves 6

455 g small prawns, peeled and deveined

120 ml olive oil plus 1 tablespoon, divided

¼ teaspoon garlic powder

¼ teaspoon cayenne

455 g whole grain pasta

5 garlic cloves, minced

230 g baby mushrooms, sliced

45 g Parmesan, plus more for serving (optional)

1 teaspoon salt

½ teaspoon black pepper

½ cup fresh basil

1. Preheat the air fryer to 192ºC. 2. In a small bowl, combine the prawns, 1 tablespoon olive oil, garlic powder, and cayenne. Toss to coat the prawns. 3. Place the prawns into the air fryer basket and roast for 5 minutes. Remove the prawns and set aside. 4. Cook the pasta according to package directions. Once done cooking, reserve ½ cup pasta water, then drain. 5. Meanwhile, in a large skillet, heat 120 ml of olive oil over medium heat. Add the garlic and mushrooms and cook down for 5 minutes. 6. Pour the pasta, reserved pasta water, Parmesan, salt, pepper, and basil into the skillet with the vegetable-and-oil mixture, and stir to coat the pasta. 7. Toss in the prawns and remove from heat, then let the mixture sit for 5 minutes before serving with additional Parmesan, if desired.

Salmon with Fennel and Carrot

Prep time: 15 minutes | Cook time: 15 minutes | Serves 4

1 fennel bulb, thinly sliced

2 large carrots, sliced

1 large onion, thinly sliced

2 teaspoons extra-virgin olive oil

120 ml sour cream

1 teaspoon dried tarragon leaves

4 x 140 g salmon fillets

⅛ teaspoon salt

¼ teaspoon coarsely ground black pepper

1. Insert the crisper plate into the basket and the basket into the unit. Preheat the unit to204ºC, 2. In a medium bowl, toss together the fennel, carrots, and onion. Add the olive oil and toss again to coat the vegetables. Put the vegetables into a 6-inch round metal pan. 3. Once the unit is preheated, place the pan into the basket. 4. Cook for 15 minutes. 5. Check after 5 minutes, the vegetables should be crisp-tender. Remove the pan and stir in the sour cream and tarragon. Top with the salmon fillets and sprinkle the fish with the salt and pepper. Reinsert the pan into the basket and resume cooking. 6. When the cooking is complete, the salmon should flake easily with a fork and a food thermometer should register at least 64ºC. Serve the salmon on top of the vegetables.

Fried Catfish Fillets

Prep time: 10 minutes | Cook time: 20 minutes | Serves 4

1 egg

100 g finely ground cornmeal

30 g plain flour

¾ teaspoon salt

1 teaspoon paprika

1 teaspoon Old Bay seasoning

¼ teaspoon garlic powder

¼ teaspoon freshly ground black pepper

4 140 g catfish fillets, halved crosswise

Olive oil spray

1. In a shallow bowl, beat the egg with 2 tablespoons water. 2. On a plate, stir together the cornmeal, flour, salt, paprika, Old Bay, garlic powder, and pepper. 3. Dip the fish into the egg mixture and into the cornmeal mixture to coat. Press the cornmeal mixture into the fish and gently shake off any excess. 4. Insert the crisper plate into the basket and the basket into the unit to 204ºC. 5. Once the unit is preheated, place a baking paper liner into the basket. Place the coated fish on the liner and spray it with olive oil.. 6. Cook for 10 minutes, remove the basket and spray the fish with olive oil. Flip the fish and spray the other side with olive oil. Reinsert the basket to resume cooking. Check the fish after 7 minutes more. If the fish is golden and crispy and registers at least 64ºC on a food thermometer, it is ready. If not, resume cooking. 8. When the cooking is complete, serve.

Steamed Tuna with Lemongrass

Prep time: 10 minutes | Cook time: 10 minutes | Serves 4

4 small tuna steaks

2 tablespoons low-sodium soy sauce

2 teaspoons sesame oil

2 teaspoons rice wine vinegar

1 teaspoon grated peeled fresh

ginger

⅛ teaspoon freshly ground black pepper

1 stalk lemongrass, bent in half

3 tablespoons freshly squeezed lemon juice

1. Place the tuna steaks on a plate. 2. In a small bowl, whisk the soy sauce, sesame oil, vinegar, and ginger until combined. Pour this mixture over the tuna and gently rub it into both sides. Sprinkle the fish with the pepper. Let marinate for 10 minutes. 3. Insert the crisper plate into the basket and the basket into the unit. Preheat the unit to 200ºC. 4. Once the unit is preheated, place the lemongrass into the basket and top it with the tuna steaks. Drizzle the tuna with the lemon juice and 1 tablespoon of water. 5. Cook for 10 minutes. 6. When the cooking is complete, a food thermometer inserted into the tuna should register at least 64ºC. Discard the lemongrass and serve the tuna.

Scallops with Asparagus and Peas

Prep time: 10 minutes | Cook time: 7 to 10 minutes | Serves 4

Cooking oil spray

455 g asparagus, ends trimmed, cut into 2-inch pieces

100 g sugar snap peas

455 g sea scallops

1 tablespoon freshly squeezed

lemon juice

2 teaspoons extra-virgin olive oil

½ teaspoon dried thyme

Salt and freshly ground black pepper, to taste

1. Insert the crisper plate into the basket and the basket into the unit. Preheat the unit to 204ºC. 2. Once the unit is preheated, spray the crisper plate with cooking oil. Place the asparagus and sugar snap peas into the basket. 3. Cook for 10 minutes. 4. Meanwhile, check the scallops for a small muscle attached to the side. Pull it off and discard. In a medium bowl, toss together the scallops, lemon juice, olive oil, and thyme. Season with salt and pepper. 5. After 3 minutes, the vegetables should be just starting to get tender. Place the scallops on top of the vegetables. Reinsert the basket to resume cooking. After 3 minutes more, remove the basket and shake it. Again reinsert the basket to resume cooking. 6. When the cooking is complete, the scallops should be firm when tested with your finger and opaque in the center, and the vegetables tender. Serve immediately.

Tandoori-Spiced Salmon and Potatoes

Prep time: 10 minutes | Cook time: 28 minutes | Serves 2

455 g Fingerling or new potatoes

2 tablespoons vegetable oil, divided

Kosher or coarse sea salt and freshly ground black pepper, to taste

1 teaspoon ground turmeric

1 teaspoon ground cumin

1 teaspoon ground ginger

½ teaspoon smoked paprika

¼ teaspoon cayenne pepper

2 x 170 g skin-on salmon fillets

1. Preheat the air fryer to 192ºC. 2. In a bowl, toss the potatoes with 1 tablespoon of the oil until evenly coated. Season with salt and pepper. Transfer the potatoes to the air fryer and air fry for 20 minutes. 3. Meanwhile, in a bowl, combine the remaining 1 tablespoon oil, the turmeric, cumin, ginger, paprika, and cayenne. Add the salmon fillets and turn in the spice mixture until fully coated all over. 4. After the potatoes have cooked for 20 minutes, place the salmon fillets, skin-side up, on top of the potatoes, and continue cooking until the potatoes are tender, the salmon is cooked, and the salmon skin is slightly crisp. 5. Transfer the salmon fillets to two plates and serve with the potatoes while both are warm.

Crab and Bell Pepper Cakes

Prep time: 5 minutes | Cook time: 10 minutes | Serves 4

230 g jumbo lump crabmeat

1 tablespoon Old Bay seasoning

40 g bread crumbs

40 g diced red bell pepper

40 g diced green bell pepper

1 egg

60 g mayonnaise

Juice of ½ lemon

1 teaspoon plain flour

Cooking oil spray

1. Sort through the crabmeat, picking out any bits of shell or cartilage. 2. In a large bowl, stir together the Old Bay seasoning, bread crumbs, red and green bell peppers, egg, mayonnaise, and lemon juice. Gently stir in the crabmeat. 3. Insert the crisper plate into the basket and the basket into the unit. Preheat the unit to 192ºC. 4. Form the mixture into 4 patties. Sprinkle ¼ teaspoon of flour on top of each patty. 5. Once the unit is preheated, spray the crisper plate with cooking oil. Place the crab cakes into the basket and spray them with cooking oil. 6. Cook for 10 minutes. 7. When the cooking is complete, the crab cakes will be golden brown and firm.

Cornmeal-Crusted Trout Fingers

Prep time: 15 minutes | Cook time: 6 minutes | Serves 2

70 g yellow cornmeal, medium or finely ground (not coarse)

40 g plain flour

1½ teaspoons baking powder

1 teaspoon kosher or coarse sea salt, plus more as needed

½ teaspoon freshly ground black pepper, plus more as needed

⅛ teaspoon cayenne pepper

340 g skinless trout fillets, cut

into strips 1 inch wide and 3 inches long

3 large eggs, lightly beaten

Cooking spray

115 g mayonnaise

2 tablespoons capers, rinsed and finely chopped

1 tablespoon fresh tarragon

1 teaspoon fresh lemon juice, plus lemon wedges, for serving

1. Preheat the air fryer to 204ºC. 2. In a large bowl, whisk together the cornmeal, flour, baking powder, salt, black pepper, and cayenne. Dip the trout strips in the egg, then toss them in the cornmeal mixture until fully coated. Transfer the trout to a rack set over a baking sheet and liberally spray all over with cooking spray. 3. Transfer half the fish to the air fryer and air fry until the fish is cooked through and golden brown, about 6 minutes. Transfer the fish sticks to a plate and repeat with the remaining fish. 4. Meanwhile, in a bowl, whisk together the mayonnaise, capers, tarragon, and lemon juice. Season the tartar sauce with salt and black pepper. 5. Serve the trout fingers hot along with the tartar sauce and lemon wedges.

Crispy Prawns with Coriander

Prep time: 40 minutes | Cook time: 10 minutes | Serves 4

455 g raw large prawns, peeled and deveined with tails on or off
30 g chopped fresh coriander
Juice of 1 lime
70 g plain flour
1 egg
75 g bread crumbs
Salt and freshly ground black pepper, to taste
Cooking oil spray
240 ml seafood sauce

1. Place the prawns in a resealable plastic bag and add the cilantro and lime juice. Seal the bag. Shake it to combine. Marinate the prawns in the refrigerator for 30 minutes. 2. Place the flour in a small bowl. 3. In another small bowl, beat the egg. 4. Place the bread crumbs in a third small bowl, season with salt and pepper, and stir to combine. 5. Insert the crisper plate into the basket and the basket into the unit. Preheat the unit to 204°C.6. Remove the prawns from the plastic bag. Dip each in the flour, the egg, and the bread crumbs to coat. Gently press the crumbs onto the prawns. 7. Once the unit is preheated, spray the crisper plate and the basket with cooking oil. Place the prawns in the basket. It is okay to stack them. Spray the prawns with the cooking oil. 8. Cook for 4 minutes, remove the basket and flip the prawns one at a time. Reinsert the basket to resume cooking. 10. When the cooking is complete, the prawns should be crisp. Let cool for 5 minutes. Serve with cocktail sauce.

Coconut Prawns with Pineapple-Lemon Sauce

Prep time: 10 minutes | Cook time: 18 minutes | Serves 4

100 g light brown sugar
2 teaspoons cornflour
⅛ teaspoon plus ½ teaspoon salt, divided
110 g crushed pineapple with syrup
2 tablespoons freshly squeezed lemon juice
1 tablespoon yellow mustard
680 g raw large prawns, peeled and deveined
2 eggs
60 g plain flour
95 g desiccated, unsweetened coconut
¼ teaspoon garlic granules
Olive oil spray

1. In a medium saucepan over medium heat, combine the brown sugar, cornflour, and ⅛ teaspoon of salt. 2. As the brown sugar mixture melts into a sauce, stir in the crushed pineapple with syrup, lemon juice, and mustard. Cook for about 4 minutes until the mixture thickens and begins to boil. Boil for 1 minute. Remove the pan from the heat, set aside, and let cool while you make the prawns. 3. Put the prawns on a plate and pat them dry with paper towels. 4. In a small bowl, whisk the eggs. 5. In a medium bowl,

stir together the flour, desiccated coconut, remaining ½ teaspoon of salt, and garlic granules. 6. Insert the crisper plate into the basket and the basket into the unit. Preheat the unit to 204°C. 7. Dip the prawns into the egg and into the coconut mixture to coat. 8. Once the unit is preheated, place a baking paper liner into the basket. Place the coated prawns on the liner in a single layer and spray them with olive oil. 9. After 6 minutes, remove the basket, flip the prawns, and spray them with more olive oil. Reinsert the basket to resume cooking. Check the prawns after 3 minutes more. If browned, they are done; if not, resume cooking. 10. When the cooking is complete, serve with the prepared pineapple sauce.

Swordfish Skewers with Caponata

Prep time: 15 minutes | Cook time: 20 minutes | Serves 2

280 g small Italian aubergine, cut into 1-inch pieces
170 g cherry tomatoes
3 spring onions, cut into 2 inches long
2 tablespoons extra-virgin olive oil, divided
Salt and pepper, to taste
340 g skinless swordfish steaks, 1¼ inches thick, cut into 1-inch pieces
2 teaspoons honey, divided
2 teaspoons ground coriander, divided
1 teaspoon grated lemon zest, divided
1 teaspoon juice
4 (6-inch) wooden skewers
1 garlic clove, minced
½ teaspoon ground cumin
1 tablespoon chopped fresh basil

1. Preheat the air fryer to 204°C. 2. Toss aubergine, tomatoes, and spring onions with 1 tablespoon oil, ¼ teaspoon salt, and ⅛ teaspoon pepper in bowl; transfer to air fryer basket. Air fry until aubergine is softened and browned and tomatoes have begun to burst, about 14 minutes, tossing halfway through cooking. Transfer vegetables to cutting board and set aside to cool slightly. 3. Pat swordfish dry with paper towels. Combine 1 teaspoon oil, 1 teaspoon honey, 1 teaspoon coriander, ½ teaspoon lemon zest, ⅛ teaspoon salt, and pinch pepper in a clean bowl. Add swordfish and toss to coat. Thread swordfish onto skewers, leaving about ¼ inch between each piece (3 or 4 pieces per skewer). 4. Arrange skewers in air fryer basket, spaced evenly apart. (Skewers may overlap slightly.) Return basket to air fryer and air fry until swordfish is browned and registers 140°F (60°C), 6 to 8 minutes, flipping and rotating skewers halfway through cooking. 5. Meanwhile, combine remaining 2 teaspoons oil, remaining 1 teaspoon honey, remaining 1 teaspoon coriander, remaining ½ teaspoon lemon zest, lemon juice, garlic, cumin, ¼ teaspoon salt, and ⅛ teaspoon pepper in large bowl. Microwave, stirring once, until fragrant, about 30 seconds. Coarsely chop the cooked vegetables, transfer to bowl with dressing, along with any accumulated juices, and gently toss to combine. Stir in basil and season with salt and pepper to taste. Serve skewers with caponata.

Thai Prawn Skewers with Peanut Dipping Sauce

Prep time: 15 minutes | Cook time: 6 minutes | Serves 2

Salt and pepper, to taste
340 g extra-large prawns, peeled and deveined
1 tablespoon vegetable oil
1 teaspoon honey
½ teaspoon grated lime zest plus 1 tablespoon juice, plus lime wedges for serving

6 (6-inch) wooden skewers
3 tablespoons creamy peanut butter
3 tablespoons hot tap water
1 tablespoon chopped fresh coriander
1 teaspoon fish sauce

1. Preheat the air fryer to 204ºC. 2. Dissolve 2 tablespoons salt in 1 litre cold water in a large container. Add prawns, cover, and refrigerate for 15 minutes. 3. Remove prawns from brine and pat dry with paper towels. Whisk oil, honey, lime zest, and ¼ teaspoon pepper together in a large bowl. Add prawns and toss to coat. Thread prawns onto skewers, leaving about ¼ inch between each prawns (3 or 4 prawns per skewer). 4. Arrange 3 skewers in air fryer basket, parallel to each other and spaced evenly apart. Arrange remaining 3 skewers on top, perpendicular to the bottom layer. Air fry until prawns are opaque throughout, 6 to 8 minutes, flipping and rotating skewers halfway through cooking. 5. Whisk peanut butter, hot tap water, lime juice, coriander, and fish sauce together in a bowl until smooth. Serve skewers with peanut dipping sauce and lime wedges.

Confetti Salmon Burgers

Prep time: 10 minutes | Cook time: 12 minutes | Serves 4

400 g cooked fresh or canned salmon, flaked with a fork
40 g minced spring onions, white and light green parts only
40 g minced red bell pepper
40 g minced celery
2 small lemons
1 teaspoon crab boil seasoning

such as Old Bay
½ teaspoon kosher or coarse sea salt
½ teaspoon black pepper
1 egg, beaten
30 g fresh bread crumbs
Vegetable oil, for spraying

1. In a large bowl, combine the salmon, vegetables, the zest and juice of 1 of the lemons, crab boil seasoning, salt, and pepper. Add the egg and bread crumbs and stir to combine. Form the mixture into 4 patties weighing approximately 140 g each. Chill until firm, about 15 minutes. 2. Preheat the air fryer to 204ºC. 3. Spray the salmon patties with oil on all sides and spray the air fryer basket to prevent sticking. Air fry for 12 minutes, flipping halfway through, until the burgers are browned and cooked through. Cut the remaining lemon into 4 wedges and serve with the burgers.

Roasted Salmon Fillets

Prep time: 5 minutes | Cook time: 10 minutes | Serves 2

2 x 230 g skin-on salmon fillets, 1½ inches thick
1 teaspoon vegetable oil

Salt and pepper, to taste
Vegetable oil spray

1. Preheat the air fryer to 204ºC. 2. Make foil sling for air fryer basket by folding 1 long sheet of aluminum foil so it is 4 inches wide. Lay sheet of foil widthwise across basket, pressing foil into and up sides of basket. Fold excess foil as needed so that edges of foil are flush with top of basket. Lightly spray foil and basket with vegetable oil spray. 3. Pat salmon dry with paper towels, rub with oil, and season with salt and pepper. Arrange fillets skin side down on sling in prepared basket, spaced evenly apart. Air fry salmon until center is still translucent when checked with the tip of a paring knife and registers 52ºC (for medium-rare), 10 to 14 minutes, using sling to rotate fillets halfway through cooking. 4. Using the sling, carefully remove salmon from air fryer. Slide fish spatula along underside of fillets and transfer to individual serving plates, leaving skin behind. Serve.

Orange-Mustard Glazed Salmon

Prep time: 10 minutes | Cook time: 10 minutes | Serves 2

1 tablespoon orange marmalade
¼ teaspoon grated orange zest plus 1 tablespoon juice
2 teaspoons whole-grain mustard

2 x 230 g skin-on salmon fillets, 1½ inches thick
Salt and pepper, to taste
Vegetable oil spray

1. Preheat the air fryer to 204ºC. 2. Make foil sling for air fryer basket by folding 1 long sheet of aluminum foil so it is 4 inches wide. Lay sheet of foil widthwise across basket, pressing foil into and up sides of basket. Fold excess foil as needed so that edges of foil are flush with top of basket. Lightly spray foil and basket with vegetable oil spray. 3. Combine marmalade, orange zest and juice, and mustard in bowl. Pat salmon dry with paper towels and season with salt and pepper. Brush tops and sides of fillets evenly with glaze. Arrange fillets skin side down on sling in prepared basket, spaced evenly apart. Air fry salmon until center is still translucent when checked with the tip of a paring knife and registers 52ºC (for medium-rare), 10 to 14 minutes, using sling to rotate fillets halfway through cooking. 4. Using the sling, carefully remove salmon from air fryer. Slide fish spatula along underside of fillets and transfer to individual serving plates, leaving skin behind. Serve.

Oyster Po'Boy

Prep time: 20 minutes | Cook time: 5 minutes | Serves 4

105 g plain flour
40 g yellow cornmeal
1 tablespoon Cajun seasoning
1 teaspoon salt
2 large eggs, beaten
1 teaspoon hot sauce
455 g pre-shucked oysters

1 (12-inch) French baguette, quartered and sliced horizontally
Tartar Sauce, as needed
150 g shredded lettuce, divided
2 tomatoes, cut into slices
Cooking spray

1. In a shallow bowl, whisk the flour, cornmeal, Cajun seasoning, and salt until blended. In a second shallow bowl, whisk together the eggs and hot sauce. 2. One at a time, dip the oysters in the cornmeal mixture, the eggs, and again in the cornmeal, coating thoroughly. 3. Preheat the air fryer to 204°C. Line the air fryer basket with baking paper. 4. Place the oysters on the baking paper and spritz with oil. 5. Air fry for 2 minutes. Shake the basket, spritz the oysters with oil, and air fry for 3 minutes more until lightly browned and crispy. 6. Spread each sandwich half with Tartar Sauce. Assemble the po'boys by layering each sandwich with fried oysters, ½ cup shredded lettuce, and 2 tomato slices. 7. Serve immediately.

Trout Amandine with Lemon Butter Sauce

Prep time: 20 minutes | Cook time:8 minutes | Serves 4

Trout Amandine:
65 g toasted almonds
30 g grated Parmesan cheese
1 teaspoon salt
½ teaspoon freshly ground black pepper
2 tablespoons butter, melted
4 x 110 g trout fillets, or salmon fillets
Cooking spray

Lemon Butter Sauce:
8 tablespoons butter, melted
2 tablespoons freshly squeezed lemon juice
½ teaspoon Worcestershire sauce
½ teaspoon salt
½ teaspoon freshly ground black pepper
¼ teaspoon hot sauce

1. In a blender or food processor, pulse the almonds for 5 to 10 seconds until finely processed. Transfer to a shallow bowl and whisk in the Parmesan cheese, salt, and pepper. Place the melted butter in another shallow bowl. 2. One at a time, dip the fish in the melted butter, then the almond mixture, coating thoroughly. 3. Preheat the air fryer to 150°C. Line the air fryer basket with baking paper. 4. Place the coated fish on the baking paper and spritz with oil. 5. Bake for 4 minutes. Flip the fish, spritz it with oil, and bake for 4 minutes more until the fish flakes easily with a fork. 6. In a small bowl, whisk the butter, lemon juice, Worcestershire sauce, salt, pepper, and hot sauce until blended. 7. Serve with the fish.

New Orleans-Style Crab Cakes

Prep time: 10 minutes | Cook time: 8 to 10 minutes | Serves 4

190 g bread crumbs
2 teaspoons Creole Seasoning
1 teaspoon dry mustard
1 teaspoon salt
1 teaspoon freshly ground black pepper

360 g crab meat
2 large eggs, beaten
1 teaspoon butter, melted
⅓ cup minced onion
Cooking spray
Tartar Sauce, for serving

1. Preheat the air fryer to 176°C. Line the air fryer basket with baking paper. 2. In a medium bowl, whisk the bread crumbs, Creole Seasoning, dry mustard, salt, and pepper until blended. Add the crab meat, eggs, butter, and onion. Stir until blended. Shape the crab mixture into 8 patties. 3. Place the crab cakes on the baking paper and spritz with oil. 4. Air fry for 4 minutes. Flip the cakes, spritz them with oil, and air fry for 4 to 6 minutes more until the outsides are firm and a fork inserted into the center comes out clean. Serve with the Tartar Sauce.

Fish Sandwich with Tartar Sauce

Prep time: 10 minutes | Cook time: 17 minutes | Serves 2

Tartar Sauce:
115 g mayonnaise
2 tablespoons onion granules
1 dill pickle spear, finely chopped
2 teaspoons pickle juice
¼ teaspoon salt
⅛ teaspoon ground black pepper

Fish:
2 tablespoons plain flour
1 egg, lightly beaten
120 g panko
2 teaspoons lemon pepper
2 tilapia fillets
Cooking spray
2 soft sub rolls

1. Preheat the air fryer to 204°C. 2. In a small bowl, combine the mayonnaise, onion granules, pickle, pickle juice, salt, and pepper. 3. Whisk to combine and chill in the refrigerator while you make the fish. 4. Place a baking paper liner in the air fryer basket. 5. Scoop the flour out onto a plate; set aside. 6. Put the beaten egg in a medium shallow bowl. 7. On another plate, mix to combine the panko and lemon pepper. 8. Dredge the tilapia fillets in the flour, then dip in the egg, and then press into the panko mixture. 9. Place the prepared fillets on the liner in the air fryer in a single layer. 10. Spray lightly with cooking spray and air fry for 8 minutes. Carefully flip the fillets, spray with more cooking spray, and air fry for an additional 9 minutes, until golden and crispy. 11. Place each cooked fillet in a sub roll, top with a little bit of tartar sauce, and serve.

Moroccan Spiced Halibut with Chickpea Salad

Prep time: 15 minutes | Cook time: 12 minutes | Serves 2

¾ teaspoon ground coriander

½ teaspoon ground cumin

¼ teaspoon ground ginger

⅛ teaspoon ground cinnamon

Salt and pepper, to taste

2 x 230 g skinless halibut fillets, 1¼ inches thick

4 teaspoons extra-virgin olive oil, divided, plus extra for drizzling

425 g can chickpeas, rinsed

1 tablespoon lemon juice, plus lemon wedges for serving

1 teaspoon harissa

½ teaspoon honey

2 carrots, peeled and shredded

2 tablespoons chopped fresh mint, divided

Vegetable oil spray

1. Preheat the air fryer to 150ºC. 2. Make foil sling for air fryer basket by folding 1 long sheet of aluminum foil so it is 4 inches wide. Lay sheet of foil widthwise across basket, pressing foil into and up sides of basket. Fold excess foil as needed so that edges of foil are flush with top of basket. Lightly spray foil and basket with vegetable oil spray. 3. Combine coriander, cumin, ginger, cinnamon, ⅛ teaspoon salt, and ⅛ teaspoon pepper in a small bowl. Pat halibut dry with paper towels, rub with 1 teaspoon oil, and sprinkle all over with spice mixture. Arrange fillets skinned side down on sling in prepared basket, spaced evenly apart. Bake until halibut flakes apart when gently prodded with a paring knife and registers 60ºC, 12 to 16 minutes, using the sling to rotate fillets halfway through cooking. 4. Meanwhile, microwave chickpeas in medium bowl until heated through, about 2 minutes. Stir in remaining 1 tablespoon oil, lemon juice, harissa, honey, ⅛ teaspoon salt, and ⅛ teaspoon pepper. Add carrots and 1 tablespoon mint and toss to combine. Season with salt and pepper, to taste. 5. Using sling, carefully remove halibut from air fryer and transfer to individual plates. Sprinkle with remaining 1 tablespoon mint and drizzle with extra oil to taste. Serve with salad and lemon wedges.

Roasted Cod with Lemon-Garlic Potatoes

Prep time: 10 minutes | Cook time: 28 minutes | Serves 2

3 tablespoons unsalted butter, softened, divided

2 garlic cloves, minced

1 lemon, grated to yield 2 teaspoons zest and sliced ¼ inch thick

Salt and pepper, to taste

1 large russet potato (about 340 g), unpeeled, sliced ¼ inch thick

1 tablespoon minced fresh parsley, chives, or tarragon

2 x 230 g skinless cod fillets, 1¼ inches thick

Vegetable oil spray

1. Preheat the air fryer to 204ºC. 2. Make foil sling for air fryer basket by folding 1 long sheet of aluminum foil so it is 4 inches wide. Lay sheet of foil widthwise across basket, pressing foil into and up sides of basket. Fold excess foil as needed so that edges of foil are flush with top of basket. Lightly spray the foil and basket with vegetable oil spray. 3. Microwave 1 tablespoon butter, garlic, 1 teaspoon lemon zest, ¼ teaspoon salt, and ⅛ teaspoon pepper in a medium bowl, stirring once, until the butter is melted and the mixture is fragrant, about 30 seconds. Add the potato slices and toss to coat. Shingle the potato slices on sling in prepared basket to create 2 even layers. Air fry until potato slices are spotty brown and just tender, 16 to 18 minutes, using a sling to rotate potatoes halfway through cooking. 4. Combine the remaining 2 tablespoons butter, remaining 1 teaspoon lemon zest, and parsley in a small bowl. Pat the cod dry with paper towels and season with salt and pepper. Place the fillets, skinned-side down, on top of potato slices, spaced evenly apart. (Tuck thinner tail ends of fillets under themselves as needed to create uniform pieces.) Dot the fillets with the butter mixture and top with the lemon slices. Return the basket to the air fryer and air fry until the cod flakes apart when gently prodded with a paring knife and registers 60ºC, 12 to 15 minutes, using a sling to rotate the potato slices and cod halfway through cooking. 5. Using a sling, carefully remove potatoes and cod from air fryer. Cut the potato slices into 2 portions between fillets using fish spatula. Slide spatula along underside of potato slices and transfer with cod to individual plates. Serve.

Classic Prawns Empanadas

Prep time: 10 minutes | Cook time: 8 minutes | Serves 5

230 g raw prawns, peeled, deveined and chopped

1 small chopped red onion

1 spring onion, chopped

2 garlic cloves, minced

2 tablespoons minced red bell pepper

2 tablespoons chopped fresh coriander

½ tablespoon fresh lime juice

¼ teaspoon sweet paprika

⅛ teaspoon kosher salt

⅛ teaspoon crushed red pepper flakes (optional)

1 large egg, beaten

10 frozen Goya Empanada Discos, thawed

Cooking spray

1. In a medium bowl, combine the prawns, red onion, spring onion, garlic, bell pepper, coriander, lime juice, paprika, salt, and pepper flakes (if using). 2. In a small bowl, beat the egg with 1 teaspoon water until smooth. 3. Place an empanada disc on a work surface and put 2 tablespoons of the prawn mixture in the center. Brush the outer edges of the disc with the egg wash. Fold the disc over and gently press the edges to seal. Use a fork and press around the edges to crimp and seal completely. Brush the tops of the empanadas with the egg wash. 4. Preheat the air fryer to 192ºC. 5. Spray the bottom of the air fryer basket with cooking spray to prevent sticking. Working in batches, arrange a single layer of the empanadas in the air fryer basket and air fry for about 8 minutes, flipping halfway, until golden brown and crispy. 6. Serve hot.

Fried Catfish with Dijon Sauce

Prep time: 20 minutes | Cook time: 7 minutes | Serves 4

4 tablespoons butter, melted

2 teaspoons Worcestershire sauce, divided

1 teaspoon lemon pepper

120 g panko bread crumbs

4 x 110 g catfish fillets

Cooking spray

120 ml sour cream

1 tablespoon Dijon mustard

1. In a shallow bowl, stir together the melted butter, 1 teaspoon of Worcestershire sauce, and the lemon pepper. Place the bread crumbs in another shallow bowl. 2. One at a time, dip both sides of the fillets in the butter mixture, then the bread crumbs, coating thoroughly. 3. Preheat the air fryer to 150ºC. Line the air fryer basket with baking paper. 4. Place the coated fish on the baking paper and spritz with oil. 5. Bake for 4 minutes. Flip the fish, spritz it with oil, and bake for 3 to 6 minutes more, depending on the thickness of the fillets, until the fish flakes easily with a fork. 6. In a small bowl, stir together the sour cream, Dijon, and remaining 1 teaspoon of Worcestershire sauce. This sauce can be made 1 day in advance and refrigerated before serving. Serve with the fried fish.

Jalea

Prep time: 20 minutes | Cook time: 10 minutes | Serves 4

Salsa Criolla:

½ red onion, thinly sliced

2 tomatoes, diced

1 serrano or jalapeño pepper, deseeded and diced

1 clove garlic, minced

5 g chopped fresh coriander

Pinch of kosher or coarse sea salt

3 limes

Fried Seafood:

455 g firm, white-fleshed fish such as cod (add an extra 230 g fish if not using prawns)

20 large or jumbo prawns, peeled and deveined

30 g plain flour

40 g cornflour

1 teaspoon garlic powder

1 teaspoon kosher or coarse sea salt

¼ teaspoon cayenne pepper

240 g panko bread crumbs

2 eggs, beaten with 2 tablespoons water

Vegetable oil, for spraying

Mayonnaise or tartar sauce, for serving (optional)

1. To make the Salsa Criolla, combine the red onion, tomatoes, pepper, garlic, cilantro, and salt in a medium bowl. Add the juice and zest of 2 of the limes. Refrigerate the salad while you make the fish. 2. To make the seafood, cut the fish fillets into strips approximately 2 inches long and 1 inch wide. Place the flour, cornstarch, garlic powder, salt, and cayenne pepper on a plate and whisk to combine. Place the panko on a separate plate. Dredge the fish strips in the seasoned flour mixture, shaking off any excess. Dip the strips in the egg mixture, coating them completely, then dredge in the panko, shaking off any excess. Place the fish strips on a plate or rack. Repeat with the prawns, if using. 3. Spray the air fryer basket with oil, and preheat the air fryer to 204ºC. Working in 2 or 3 batches, arrange the fish and prawns in a single layer in the basket, taking care not to crowd the basket. Spray with oil. Air fry for 5 minutes, then flip and air fry for another 4 to 5 minutes until the outside is brown and crisp and the inside of the fish is opaque and flakes easily with a fork. Repeat with the remaining seafood. 4. Place the fried seafood on a platter. Use a slotted spoon to remove the salsa criolla from the bowl, leaving behind any liquid that has accumulated. Place the salsa criolla on top of the fried seafood. Serve immediately with the remaining lime, cut into wedges, and mayonnaise or tartar sauce as desired.

Tuna-Stuffed Quinoa Patties

Prep time: 10 minutes | Cook time: 15 minutes | Serves 4

35 g quinoa

4 slices white bread with crusts removed

120 ml milk

3 eggs

280 g tuna packed in olive oil, drained

2 to 3 lemons

Kosher or coarse sea salt, and pepper, to taste

150 g panko bread crumbs

Vegetable oil, for spraying

Lemon wedges, for serving

1. Rinse the quinoa in a fine-mesh sieve until the water runs clear. Bring 1 liter of salted water to a boil. Add the quinoa, cover, and reduce heat to low. Simmer the quinoa covered until most of the water is absorbed and the quinoa is tender, 15 to 20 minutes. Drain and allow to cool to room temperature. Meanwhile, soak the bread in the milk. 2. Mix the drained quinoa with the soaked bread and 2 of the eggs in a large bowl and mix thoroughly. In a medium bowl, combine the tuna, the remaining egg, and the juice and zest of 1 of the lemons. Season well with salt and pepper. Spread the panko on a plate. 3. Scoop up approximately 60 g of the quinoa mixture and flatten into a patty. Place a heaping tablespoon of the tuna mixture in the center of the patty and close the quinoa around the tuna. Flatten the patty slightly to create an oval-shaped croquette. Dredge both sides of the croquette in the panko. Repeat with the remaining quinoa and tuna. 4. Spray the air fryer basket with oil to prevent sticking, and preheat the air fryer to 204ºC. Arrange 4 or 5 of the croquettes in the basket, taking care to avoid overcrowding. Spray the tops of the croquettes with oil. Air fry for 8 minutes until the top side is browned and crispy. Carefully turn the croquettes over and spray the second side with oil. Air fry until the second side is browned and crispy, another 7 minutes. Repeat with the remaining croquettes. 5. Serve the croquetas warm with plenty of lemon wedges for spritzing.

Sole and Asparagus Bundles

Prep time: 10 minutes | Cook time: 14 minutes | Serves 2

230 g asparagus, trimmed
1 teaspoon extra-virgin olive oil, divided
Salt and pepper, to taste
4 x 85 g skinless sole fillets, ⅛ to ¼ inch thick
4 tablespoons unsalted butter, softened
1 small shallot, minced
1 tablespoon chopped fresh tarragon
¼ teaspoon lemon zest plus ½ teaspoon juice
Vegetable oil spray

1. Preheat the air fryer to 150ºC. 2. Toss asparagus with ½ teaspoon oil, pinch salt, and pinch pepper in a bowl. Cover and microwave until bright green and just tender, about 3 minutes, tossing halfway through microwaving. Uncover and set aside to cool slightly. 3. Make foil sling for air fryer basket by folding 1 long sheet of aluminum foil so it is 4 inches wide. Lay sheet of foil widthwise across basket, pressing foil into and up sides of basket. Fold excess foil as needed so that edges of foil are flush with top of basket. Lightly spray foil and basket with vegetable oil spray. 4. Pat sole dry with paper towels and season with salt and pepper. Arrange fillets skinned side up on cutting board, with thicker ends closest to you. Arrange asparagus evenly across base of each fillet, then tightly roll fillets away from you around asparagus to form tidy bundles. 5. Rub bundles evenly with remaining ½ teaspoon oil and arrange seam side down on sling in prepared basket. Bake until asparagus is tender and sole flakes apart when gently prodded with a paring knife, 14 to 18 minutes, using a sling to rotate bundles halfway through cooking. 6. Combine butter, shallot, tarragon, and lemon zest and juice in a bowl. Using sling, carefully remove sole bundles from air fryer and transfer to individual plates. Top evenly with butter mixture and serve.

Crab Cakes with Lettuce and Apple Salad

Prep time: 10 minutes | Cook time: 13 minutes | Serves 2

230 g lump crab meat, picked over for shells
2 tablespoons panko bread crumbs
1 spring onions, minced
1 large egg
1 tablespoon mayonnaise
1½ teaspoons Dijon mustard
Pinch of cayenne pepper
2 shallots, sliced thin
1 tablespoon extra-virgin olive oil, divided
1 teaspoon lemon juice, plus lemon wedges for serving
⅛ teaspoon salt
Pinch of pepper
85 g small head round lettuce, torn into bite-size pieces
½ apple, cored and sliced thin

1. Preheat the air fryer to 204ºC. 2. Line large plate with triple layer of paper towels. Transfer crab meat to prepared plate and pat dry with additional paper towels. Combine panko, spring onion, egg, mayonnaise, mustard, and cayenne in a bowl. Using a rubber spatula, gently fold in crab meat until combined; discard paper towels. Divide crab mixture into 4 tightly packed balls, then flatten each into 1-inch-thick cake (cakes will be delicate). Transfer cakes to plate and refrigerate until firm, about 10 minutes. 3. Toss shallots with ½ teaspoon oil in separate bowl; transfer to air fryer basket. Air fry until shallots are browned, 5 to 7 minutes, tossing once halfway through cooking. Return shallots to now-empty bowl and set aside. 4. Arrange crab cakes in air fryer basket, spaced evenly apart. Return basket to air fryer and air fry until crab cakes are light golden brown on both sides, 8 to 10 minutes, flipping and rotating cakes halfway through cooking. 5. Meanwhile, whisk remaining 2½ teaspoons oil, lemon juice, salt, and pepper together in large bowl. Add lettuce, apple, and shallots and toss to coat. Serve crab cakes with salad, passing lemon wedges separately.

Crunchy Air Fried Cod Fillets

Prep time: 10 minutes | Cook time: 12 minutes | Serves 2

40 g panko bread crumbs
1 teaspoon vegetable oil
1 small shallot, minced
1 small garlic clove, minced
½ teaspoon minced fresh thyme
Salt and pepper, to taste
1 tablespoon minced fresh parsley
1 tablespoon mayonnaise
1 large egg yolk
¼ teaspoon grated lemon zest, plus lemon wedges for serving
2 x 230 g skinless cod fillets, 1¼ inches thick
Vegetable oil spray

1. Preheat the air fryer to 150ºC. 2. Make foil sling for air fryer basket by folding 1 long sheet of aluminum foil so it is 4 inches wide. Lay sheet of foil widthwise across basket, pressing foil into and up sides of basket. Fold excess foil as needed so that edges of foil are flush with top of basket. Lightly spray the foil and basket with vegetable oil spray. 3. Toss the panko with the oil in a bowl until evenly coated. Stir in the shallot, garlic, thyme, ¼ teaspoon salt, and ⅛ teaspoon pepper. Microwave, stirring frequently, until the panko is light golden brown, about 2 minutes. Transfer to a shallow dish and let cool slightly; stir in the parsley. Whisk the mayonnaise, egg yolk, lemon zest, and ⅛ teaspoon pepper together in another bowl. 4. Pat the cod dry with paper towels and season with salt and pepper. Arrange the fillets, skinned-side down, on plate and brush tops evenly with mayonnaise mixture. (Tuck thinner tail ends of fillets under themselves as needed to create uniform pieces.) Working with 1 fillet at a time, dredge the coated side in panko mixture, pressing gently to adhere. Arrange the fillets, crumb-side up, on sling in the prepared basket, spaced evenly apart. 5. Bake for 12 to 16 minutes, using a sling to rotate fillets halfway through cooking. Using a sling, carefully remove cod from air fryer. Serve with the lemon wedges.

Pecan-Crusted Tilapia

Prep time: 10minutes | Cook time: 10 minutes | Serves 4

160 g pecans	tablespoons water
45 g panko bread crumbs	4 x 170 g tilapia fillets
70 g plain flour	Vegetable oil, for spraying
2 tablespoons Cajun seasoning	Lemon wedges, for serving
2 eggs, beaten with 2	

1. Grind the pecans in the food processor until they resemble coarse meal. Combine the ground pecans with the panko on a plate. On a second plate, combine the flour and Cajun seasoning. Dry the tilapia fillets using paper towels and dredge them in the flour mixture, shaking off any excess. Dip the fillets in the egg mixture and then dredge them in the pecan and panko mixture, pressing the coating onto the fillets. Place the breaded fillets on a plate or rack. 2. Preheat the air fryer to 192°C. Spray both sides of the breaded fillets with oil. Carefully transfer 2 of the fillets to the air fryer basket and air fry for 9 to 10 minutes, flipping once halfway through, until the flesh is opaque and flaky. Repeat with the remaining fillets. 3. Serve immediately with lemon wedges.

Crab Cakes with Sriracha Mayonnaise

Prep time: 15 minutes | Cook time: 10 minutes | Serves 4

Sriracha Mayonnaise:	40 g diced celery
230 g mayonnaise	455 g lump crab meat
1 tablespoon Sriracha	1 teaspoon Old Bay seasoning
1½ teaspoons freshly squeezed lemon juice	1 egg
Crab Cakes:	1½ teaspoons freshly squeezed lemon juice
1 teaspoon extra-virgin olive oil	200 g panko bread crumbs, divided
40 g finely diced red bell pepper	
40 g diced onion	Vegetable oil, for spraying

1. Mix the mayonnaise, Sriracha, and lemon juice in a small bowl. Place ⅔of the mixture in a separate bowl to form the base of the crab cakes. Cover the remaining Sriracha mayonnaise and refrigerate. (This will become dipping sauce for the crab cakes once they are cooked.) 2. Heat the olive oil in a heavy-bottomed, medium skillet over medium-high heat. Add the bell pepper, onion, and celery and sauté for 3 minutes. Transfer the vegetables to the bowl with the reserved ⅔ of Sriracha mayonnaise. Mix in the crab, Old Bay seasoning, egg, and lemon juice. Add 120 g of the panko. Form the crab mixture into 8 cakes. Dredge the cakes in the remaining panko, turning to coat. Place on a baking sheet. Cover and refrigerate for at least 1 hour and up to 8 hours. 3. Preheat the air fryer to 192°C. Spray the air fryer basket with oil. Working in batches as needed so as not to overcrowd the basket, place the chilled crab cakes in a single layer in the basket. Spray the crab cakes with oil. Bake until golden brown, 8 to 10 minutes, carefully turning halfway through cooking. Remove to a platter and keep warm. Repeat with the remaining crab cakes as needed. Serve the crab cakes immediately with Sriracha mayonnaise dipping sauce.

Prawn Dejonghe Skewers

Prep time: 10 minutes | Cook time: 15 minutes | Serves 4

2 teaspoons sherry, or apple cider vinegar	more for garnish
	1 teaspoon kosher salt
3 tablespoons unsalted butter, melted	Pinch of cayenne pepper
	680 g prawns, peeled and deveined
120 g panko bread crumbs	
3 cloves garlic, minced	Vegetable oil, for spraying
8 g minced flat-leaf parsley, plus	Lemon wedges, for serving

1. Stir the sherry and melted butter together in a shallow bowl or pie plate and whisk until combined. Set aside. Whisk together the panko, garlic, parsley, salt, and cayenne pepper on a large plate or shallow bowl. 2. Thread the prawns onto metal skewers designed for the air fryer or bamboo skewers, 3 to 4 per skewer. Dip 1 prawns skewer in the butter mixture, then dredge in the panko mixture until each prawns is lightly coated. Place the skewer on a plate or rimmed baking sheet and repeat the process with the remaining skewers. 3. Preheat the air fryer to 176°C. Arrange 4 skewers in the air fryer basket. Spray the skewers with oil and air fry for 8 minutes, until the bread crumbs are golden brown and the prawns are cooked through. Transfer the cooked skewers to a serving plate and keep warm while cooking the remaining 4 skewers in the air fryer. 4. Sprinkle the cooked skewers with additional fresh parsley and serve with lemon wedges if desired.

Blackened Fish

Prep time: 15 minutes | Cook time: 8 minutes | Serves 4

1 large egg, beaten	4 x 110 g tilapia fillets
Blackened seasoning, as needed	Cooking spray
2 tablespoons light brown sugar	

1. In a shallow bowl, place the beaten egg. In a second shallow bowl, stir together the Blackened seasoning and the brown sugar. 2. One at a time, dip the fish fillets in the egg, then the brown sugar mixture, coating thoroughly. 3. Preheat the air fryer to 150°C. Line the air fryer basket with baking paper. 4. Place the coated fish on the baking paper and spritz with oil. 5. Bake for 4 minutes. Flip the fish, spritz it with oil, and bake for 4 to 6 minutes more until the fish is white inside and flakes easily with a fork. 6. Serve immediately.

Lemony Prawns and Courgette

Prep time: 15 minutes | Cook time: 7 to 8 minutes | Serves 4

570 g extra-large raw prawns, peeled and deveined
2 medium courgettes (about 230 g each), halved lengthwise and cut into ½-inch-thick slices
1½ tablespoons olive oil
½ teaspoon garlic salt
1½ teaspoons dried oregano
⅛ teaspoon crushed red pepper flakes (optional)
Juice of ½ lemon
1 tablespoon chopped fresh mint
1 tablespoon chopped fresh dill

1. Preheat the air fryer to 176ºC. 2. In a large bowl, combine the prawns, courgette, oil, garlic salt, oregano, and pepper flakes (if using) and toss to coat. 3. Working in batches, arrange a single layer of the prawns and courgette in the air fryer basket. Air fry for 7 to 8 minutes, shaking the basket halfway, until the courgette is golden and the prawns are cooked through. 4. Transfer to a serving dish and tent with foil while you air fry the remaining prawns and courgette. 5. Top with the lemon juice, mint, and dill and serve.

Tortilla Prawn Tacos

Prep time: 10 minutes | Cook time: 6 minutes | Serves 4

Spicy Mayo:
3 tablespoons mayonnaise
1 tablespoon Louisiana-style hot pepper sauce, or Sriracha
Coriander-Lime Slaw:
180 g shredded green cabbage
½ small red onion, thinly sliced
1 small jalapeño, thinly sliced
2 tablespoons chopped fresh cilantro
Juice of 1 lime
¼ teaspoon kosher salt
Prawns:
1 large egg, beaten
1 cup crushed tortilla chips
24 jumbo prawns (about 455 g), peeled and deveined
⅛ teaspoon kosher or coarse sea salt
Cooking spray
8 corn tortillas, for serving

1. For the spicy mayo: In a small bowl, mix the mayonnaise and hot pepper sauce. 2. For the coriander-lime slaw: In a large bowl, toss together the cabbage, onion, jalapeño, coriander, lime juice, and salt to combine. Cover and refrigerate to chill. 3. For the prawns: Place the egg in a shallow bowl and the crushed tortilla chips in another. Season the prawns with the salt. Dip the prawns in the egg, then in the crumbs, pressing gently to adhere. Place on a work surface and spray both sides with oil. 4. Preheat the air fryer to 182ºC. 5. Working in batches, arrange a single layer of the prawns in the air fryer basket. Air fry for 6 minutes, flipping halfway, until golden and cooked through in the center. 6. To serve, place 2 tortillas on each plate and top each with 3 prawns. Top each taco with ¼ of the slaw, then drizzle with spicy mayo.

Crab Cake Sandwich

Prep time: 15 minutes | Cook time: 10 minutes | Serves 4

Crab Cakes:
60 g panko bread crumbs
1 large egg, beaten
1 large egg white
1 tablespoon mayonnaise
1 teaspoon Dijon mustard
5 g minced fresh parsley
1 tablespoon fresh lemon juice
½ teaspoon Old Bay seasoning
⅛ teaspoon sweet paprika
⅛ teaspoon kosher or coarse sea salt
Freshly ground black pepper, to taste
280 g lump crab meat
Cooking spray
Cajun Mayo:
60 g mayonnaise
1 tablespoon minced dill pickle
1 teaspoon fresh lemon juice
¾ teaspoon Cajun seasoning
For Serving:
4 round lettuce leaves
4 whole wheat potato buns or gluten-free buns

1. For the crab cakes: In a large bowl, combine the panko, whole egg, egg white, mayonnaise, mustard, parsley, lemon juice, Old Bay, paprika, salt, and pepper to taste and mix well. Fold in the crab meat, being careful not to over mix. Gently shape into 4 round patties, ¾ inch thick. Spray both sides with oil. 2. Preheat the air fryer to 188ºC. 3. Working in batches, place the crab cakes in the air fryer basket. Air fry for about 10 minutes, flipping halfway, until the edges are golden. 4. Meanwhile, for the Cajun mayo: In a small bowl, combine the mayonnaise, pickle, lemon juice, and Cajun seasoning. 5. To serve: Place a lettuce leaf on each bun bottom and top with a crab cake and a generous tablespoon of Cajun mayonnaise. Add the bun top and serve.

Fried Prawns

Prep time: 15 minutes | Cook time: 5 minutes | Serves 4

70 g self-raising flour
1 teaspoon paprika
1 teaspoon salt
½ teaspoon freshly ground black pepper
1 large egg, beaten
120 g finely crushed panko bread crumbs
20 frozen large prawns (about 900 g), peeled and deveined
Cooking spray

1. In a shallow bowl, whisk the flour, paprika, salt, and pepper until blended. Add the beaten egg to a second shallow bowl and the bread crumbs to a third. 2. One at a time, dip the prawns into the flour, the egg, and the bread crumbs, coating thoroughly. 3. Preheat the air fryer to 204ºC. Line the air fryer basket with baking paper. 4. Place the prawns on the baking paper and spritz with oil. 5. Air fry for 2 minutes. Shake the basket, spritz the prawns with oil, and air fry for 3 minutes more until lightly browned and crispy. Serve hot.

Prawn Creole Casserole

Prep time: 20 minutes | Cook time: 25 minutes | Serves 4

360 g prawns, peeled and deveined
50 g chopped celery
50 g chopped onion
50 g chopped green bell pepper
2 large eggs, beaten
240 ml single cream
1 tablespoon butter, melted

1 tablespoon cornflour
1 teaspoon Creole seasoning
¾ teaspoon salt
½ teaspoon freshly ground black pepper
120 g shredded Cheddar cheese
Cooking spray

1. In a medium bowl, stir together the prawns, celery, onion, and green pepper. 2. In another medium bowl, whisk the eggs, single cream, butter, cornflour, Creole seasoning, salt, and pepper until blended. Stir the egg mixture into the prawn mixture. Add the cheese and stir to combine. 3. Preheat the air fryer to 150°C. Spritz a baking pan with oil. 4. Transfer the prawn mixture to the prepared pan and place it in the air fryer basket. 5. Bake for 25 minutes, stirring every 10 minutes, until a knife inserted into the center comes out clean. 6. Serve immediately.

Roasted Fish with Almond-Lemon Crumbs

Prep time: 10 minutes | Cook time: 7 to 8 minutes | Serves 4

70 g raw whole almonds
1 spring onion, finely chopped
Grated zest and juice of 1 lemon
½ tablespoon extra-virgin olive oil
¾ teaspoon kosher or coarse sea salt, divided

Freshly ground black pepper, to taste
4 x 170 g skinless fish fillets
Cooking spray
1 teaspoon Dijon mustard

1. In a food processor, pulse the almonds to coarsely chop. Transfer to a small bowl and add the scallion, lemon zest, and olive oil. Season with ¼ teaspoon of the salt and pepper to taste and mix to combine. 2. Spray the top of the fish with oil and squeeze the lemon juice over the fish. Season with the remaining ½ teaspoon salt and pepper to taste. Spread the mustard on top of the fish. Dividing evenly, press the almond mixture onto the top of the fillets to adhere. 3. Preheat the air fryer to 192°C. 4. Working in batches, place the fillets in the air fryer basket in a single layer. Air fry for 7 to 8 minutes, until the crumbs start to brown and the fish is cooked through. 5. Serve immediately.

Chapter 6 Vegetables and Sides

Chapter 6 Vegetables and Sides

Creamed Asparagus

Prep time: 10 minutes | Cook time: 18 minutes | Serves 4

120 g whipping cream
45 g grated Parmesan cheese
60 g cream cheese, softened
450 g asparagus, ends trimmed,

chopped into 1-inch pieces
¼ teaspoon salt
¼ teaspoon ground black pepper

1. In a medium bowl, whisk together whipping cream, Parmesan, and cream cheese until combined. 2. Place asparagus into an ungreased round nonstick baking dish. Pour cheese mixture over top and sprinkle with salt and pepper. 3. Place dish into air fryer basket. Adjust the temperature to 180ºC and set the timer for 18 minutes. Asparagus will be tender when done. Serve warm.

Crispy Green Beans

Prep time: 5 minutes | Cook time: 8 minutes | Serves 4

2 teaspoons olive oil
230 g fresh green beans, ends trimmed

¼ teaspoon salt
¼ teaspoon ground black pepper

1. In a large bowl, drizzle olive oil over green beans and sprinkle with salt and pepper. 2. Place green beans into ungreased air fryer basket. Adjust the temperature to 180ºC and set the timer for 8 minutes, shaking the basket two times during cooking. Green beans will be dark golden and crispy at the edges when done. Serve warm.

Cheesy Cauliflower Tots

Prep time: 15 minutes | Cook time: 12 minutes | Makes 16 tots

1 large head cauliflower
225 g shredded Mozzarella cheese
45 g grated Parmesan cheese

1 large egg
¼ teaspoon garlic powder
¼ teaspoon dried parsley
⅛ teaspoon onion powder

1. On the stovetop, fill a large pot with 480 ml water and place a steamer in the pan. Bring water to a boil. Cut the cauliflower into florets and place on steamer basket. Cover pot with lid. 2. Allow cauliflower to steam 7 minutes until fork tender. Remove from steamer basket and place into cheesecloth or clean kitchen towel and let cool. Squeeze over sink to remove as much excess moisture

as possible. The mixture will be too soft to form into tots if not all the moisture is removed. Mash with a fork to a smooth consistency. 3. Put the cauliflower into a large mixing bowl and add Mozzarella, Parmesan, egg, garlic powder, parsley, and onion powder. Stir until fully combined. The mixture should be wet but easy to mold. 4. Take 2 tablespoons of the mixture and roll into tot shape. Repeat with remaining mixture. Place into the air fryer basket. 5. Adjust the temperature to 160ºC and set the timer for 12 minutes. 6. Turn tots halfway through the cooking time. Cauliflower tots should be golden when fully cooked. Serve warm.

Cauliflower with Lime Juice

Prep time: 10 minutes | Cook time: 7 minutes | Serves 4

215 g chopped cauliflower florets
2 tablespoons coconut oil, melted

2 teaspoons chili powder
½ teaspoon garlic powder
1 medium lime
2 tablespoons chopped coriander

1. In a large bowl, toss cauliflower with coconut oil. Sprinkle with chili powder and garlic powder. Place seasoned cauliflower into the air fryer basket. 2. Adjust the temperature to 180ºC and set the timer for 7 minutes. 3. Cauliflower will be tender and begin to turn golden at the edges. Place into a serving bowl. 4. Cut the lime into quarters and squeeze juice over cauliflower. Garnish with coriander.

Cheddar Broccoli with Bacon

Prep time: 10 minutes | Cook time: 10 minutes | Serves 2

215 g fresh broccoli florets
1 tablespoon coconut oil
115 g shredded sharp Cheddar cheese
60 g full-fat sour cream

4 slices sugar-free bacon, cooked and crumbled
1 spring onion, sliced on the bias

1. Place broccoli into the air fryer basket and drizzle it with coconut oil. 2. Adjust the temperature to 180ºC and set the timer for 10 minutes. 3. Toss the basket two or three times during cooking to avoid burned spots. 4. When broccoli begins to crisp at ends, remove from fryer. Top with shredded cheese, sour cream, and crumbled bacon and garnish with spring onion slices.

Broccoli with Sesame Dressing

Prep time: 5 minutes | Cook time: 10 minutes | Serves 4

425 g broccoli florets, cut into bite-size pieces	2 tablespoons coconut aminos
1 tablespoon olive oil	2 tablespoons sesame oil
¼ teaspoon salt	½ teaspoon xylitol
2 tablespoons sesame seeds	¼ teaspoon red pepper flakes (optional)
2 tablespoons rice vinegar	

1. Preheat the air fryer to 200ºC. 2. In a large bowl, toss the broccoli with the olive oil and salt until thoroughly coated. 3. Transfer the broccoli to the air fryer basket. Pausing halfway through the cooking time to shake the basket, air fry for 10 minutes until the stems are tender and the edges are beginning to crisp. 4. Meanwhile, in the same large bowl, whisk together the sesame seeds, vinegar, coconut aminos, sesame oil, xylitol, and red pepper flakes (if using). 5. Transfer the broccoli to the bowl and toss until thoroughly coated with the seasonings. Serve warm or at room temperature.

Broccoli Salad

Prep time: 5 minutes | Cook time: 7 minutes | Serves 4

140 g fresh broccoli florets, chopped	⅛ teaspoon ground black pepper
1 tablespoon olive oil	65 ml lemon juice, divided
¼ teaspoon salt	20 g shredded Parmesan cheese
	30 g sliced roasted almonds

1. In a large bowl, toss broccoli and olive oil together. Sprinkle with salt and pepper, then drizzle with 2 tablespoons lemon juice. 2. Place broccoli into ungreased air fryer basket. Adjust the temperature to 180ºC and set the timer for 7 minutes, shaking the basket halfway through cooking. Broccoli will be golden on the edges when done. 3. Place broccoli into a large serving bowl and drizzle with remaining lemon juice. Sprinkle with Parmesan and almonds. Serve warm.

Garlic Herb Radishes

Prep time: 10 minutes | Cook time: 10 minutes | Serves 4

450 g radishes	½ teaspoon dried parsley
2 tablespoons unsalted butter, melted	¼ teaspoon dried oregano
½ teaspoon garlic powder	¼ teaspoon ground black pepper

1. Remove roots from radishes and cut into quarters. 2. In a small bowl, add butter and seasonings. Toss the radishes in the herb butter and place into the air fryer basket. 3. Adjust the temperature to 180ºC and set the timer for 10 minutes. 4. Halfway through the cooking time, toss the radishes in the air fryer basket. Continue cooking until edges begin to turn brown. 5. Serve warm.

Roasted Aubergine

Prep time: 15 minutes | Cook time: 15 minutes | Serves 4

1 large aubergine	¼ teaspoon salt
2 tablespoons olive oil	½ teaspoon garlic powder

1. Remove top and bottom from aubergine. Slice aubergine into ¼-inch-thick round slices. 2. Brush slices with olive oil. Sprinkle with salt and garlic powder. Place aubergine slices into the air fryer basket. 3. Adjust the temperature to 200ºC and set the timer for 15 minutes. 4. Serve immediately.

Rosemary-Roasted Red Potatoes

Prep time: 5 minutes | Cook time: 20 minutes | Serves 6

450 g red potatoes, quartered	¼ teaspoon black pepper
65 ml olive oil	1 garlic clove, minced
½ teaspoon coarse sea salt	4 rosemary sprigs

1. Preheat the air fryer to 180ºC. 2. In a large bowl, toss the potatoes with the olive oil, salt, pepper, and garlic until well coated. 3. Pour the potatoes into the air fryer basket and top with the sprigs of rosemary. 4. Roast for 10 minutes, then stir or toss the potatoes and roast for 10 minutes more. 5. Remove the rosemary sprigs and serve the potatoes. Season with additional salt and pepper, if needed.

Spiced Honey-Walnut Carrots

Prep time: 5 minutes | Cook time: 12 minutes | Serves 6

450 g baby carrots	¼ teaspoon ground cinnamon
2 tablespoons olive oil	25 g black walnuts, chopped
80 g raw honey	

1. Preheat the air fryer to 180ºC. 2. In a large bowl, toss the baby carrots with olive oil, honey, and cinnamon until well coated. 3. Pour into the air fryer and roast for 6 minutes. Shake the basket, sprinkle the walnuts on top, and roast for 6 minutes more. 4. Remove the carrots from the air fryer and serve.

Roasted Radishes with Sea Salt

Prep time: 5 minutes | Cook time: 18 minutes | Serves 4

450 g radishes, ends trimmed if needed	2 tablespoons olive oil
	½ teaspoon sea salt

1. Preheat the air fryer to 180ºC. 2. In a large bowl, combine the radishes with olive oil and sea salt. 3. Pour the radishes into the air fryer and roast for 10 minutes. Stir or turn the radishes over and roast for 8 minutes more, then serve.

Garlic Courgette and Red Peppers

Prep time: 5 minutes | Cook time: 15 minutes | Serves 6

2 medium courgette, cubed	2 tablespoons olive oil
1 red pepper, diced	½ teaspoon salt
2 garlic cloves, sliced	

1. Preheat the air fryer to 380°F(193°C). 2. In a large bowl, mix together the courgette, bell pepper, and garlic with the olive oil and salt. 3. Pour the mixture into the air fryer basket, and roast for 7 minutes. Shake or stir, then roast for 7 to 8 minutes more.

Parmesan and Herb Sweet Potatoes

Prep time: 10 minutes | Cook time: 18 minutes | Serves 4

2 large sweet potatoes, peeled and cubed	½ teaspoon salt
65 ml olive oil	2 tablespoons shredded Parmesan
1 teaspoon dried rosemary	

1. Preheat the air fryer to 180ºC. 2. In a large bowl, toss the sweet potatoes with the olive oil, rosemary, and salt. 3. Pour the potatoes into the air fryer basket and roast for 10 minutes, then stir the potatoes and sprinkle the Parmesan over the top. Continue roasting for 8 minutes more. 4. Serve hot and enjoy.

Sausage-Stuffed Mushroom Caps

Prep time: 10 minutes | Cook time: 8 minutes | Serves 2

6 large portobello mushroom caps	2 tablespoons blanched finely ground almond flour
230 g Italian sausage	20 g grated Parmesan cheese
15 g chopped onion	1 teaspoon minced fresh garlic

1. Use a spoon to hollow out each mushroom cap, reserving scrapings. 2. In a medium skillet over medium heat, brown the sausage about 10 minutes or until fully cooked and no pink remains. Drain and then add reserved mushroom scrapings, onion, almond flour, Parmesan, and garlic. Gently fold ingredients together and continue cooking an additional minute, then remove from heat. 3. Evenly spoon the mixture into mushroom caps and place the caps into a 6-inch round pan. Place pan into the air fryer basket. 4. Adjust the temperature to 192ºC and set the timer for 8 minutes. 5. When finished cooking, the tops will be browned and bubbling. Serve warm.

Shishito Pepper Roast

Prep time: 4 minutes | Cook time: 9 minutes | Serves 4

Cooking oil spray (sunflower, safflower, or refined coconut)	1 tablespoon soy sauce
450 g shishito, Anaheim, or bell peppers, rinsed	2 teaspoons freshly squeezed lime juice
	2 large garlic cloves, pressed

1. Insert the crisper plate into the basket and the basket into the unit. Preheat the unit by selecting AIR ROAST, setting the temperature to 200ºC, and setting the time to 3 minutes. Select START/STOP to begin. 2. Once the unit is preheated, spray the crisper plate and the basket with cooking oil. Place the peppers into the basket and spray them with oil. 3. Select AIR ROAST, set the temperature to 200ºC, and set the time to 9 minutes. Select START/STOP to begin. 4. After 3 minutes, remove the basket and shake the peppers. Spray the peppers with more oil. Reinsert the basket to resume cooking. Repeat this step again after 3 minutes. 5. While the peppers roast, in a medium bowl, whisk the soy sauce, lime juice, and garlic until combined. Set aside. 6. When the cooking is complete, several of the peppers should have lots of nice browned spots on them. If using Anaheim or bell peppers, cut a slit in the side of each pepper and remove the seeds, which can be bitter. 7. Place the roasted peppers in the bowl with the sauce. Toss to coat the peppers evenly and serve.

Dill-and-Garlic Beetroots

Prep time: 10 minutes | Cook time: 30 minutes | Serves 4

4 beetroots, cleaned, peeled, and sliced	¼ teaspoon salt
1 garlic clove, minced	¼ teaspoon black pepper
2 tablespoons chopped fresh dill	3 tablespoons olive oil

1. Preheat the air fryer to 192ºC. 2. In a large bowl, mix together all of the ingredients so the beetroots are well coated with the oil. 3. Pour the beetroot mixture into the air fryer basket, and roast for 15 minutes before stirring, then continue roasting for 15 minutes more.

Roasted Brussels Sprouts with Orange and Garlic

Prep time: 5 minutes | Cook time: 10 minutes | Serves 4

450 g Brussels sprouts, quartered

2 garlic cloves, minced

2 tablespoons olive oil

½ teaspoon salt

1 orange, cut into rings

1. Preheat the air fryer to 180ºC. 2. In a large bowl, toss the quartered Brussels sprouts with the garlic, olive oil, and salt until well coated. 3. Pour the Brussels sprouts into the air fryer, lay the orange slices on top of them, and roast for 10 minutes. 4. Remove from the air fryer and set the orange slices aside. Toss the Brussels sprouts before serving.

Citrus-Roasted Broccoli Florets

Prep time: 5 minutes | Cook time: 12 minutes | Serves 6

285 g broccoli florets (approximately 1 large head)

2 tablespoons olive oil

½ teaspoon salt

130 ml orange juice

1 tablespoon raw honey

Orange wedges, for serving (optional)

1. Preheat the air fryer to 180ºC. 2. In a large bowl, combine the broccoli, olive oil, salt, orange juice, and honey. Toss the broccoli in the liquid until well coated. 3. Pour the broccoli mixture into the air fryer basket and roast for 6 minutes. Stir and roast for 6 minutes more. 4. Serve alone or with orange wedges for additional citrus flavour, if desired.

Crispy Lemon Artichoke Hearts

Prep time: 10 minutes | Cook time: 15 minutes | Serves 2

1 (425 g) can artichoke hearts in water, drained

1 egg

1 tablespoon water

30 g whole wheat bread crumbs

¼ teaspoon salt

¼ teaspoon paprika

½ lemon

1. Preheat the air fryer to 192ºC. 2. In a medium shallow bowl, beat together the egg and water until frothy. 3. In a separate medium shallow bowl, mix together the bread crumbs, salt, and paprika. 4. Dip each artichoke heart into the egg mixture, then into the bread crumb mixture, coating the outside with the crumbs. Place the artichokes hearts in a single layer of the air fryer basket. 5. Fry the artichoke hearts for 15 minutes. 6. Remove the artichokes from the air fryer, and squeeze fresh lemon juice over the top before serving.

Stuffed Red Peppers with Herbed Ricotta and Tomatoes

Prep time: 10 minutes | Cook time: 20 minutes | Serves 4

2 red peppers

250 g cooked brown rice

2 plum tomatoes, diced

1 garlic clove, minced

¼ teaspoon salt

¼ teaspoon black pepper

115 g ricotta

3 tablespoons fresh basil, chopped

3 tablespoons fresh oregano, chopped

20 g shredded Parmesan, for topping

1. Preheat the air fryer to 180ºC. 2. Cut the bell peppers in half and remove the seeds and stem. 3. In a medium bowl, combine the brown rice, tomatoes, garlic, salt, and pepper. 4. Distribute the rice filling evenly among the four bell pepper halves. 5. In a small bowl, combine the ricotta, basil, and oregano. Put the herbed cheese over the top of the rice mixture in each bell pepper. 6. Place the bell peppers into the air fryer and roast for 20 minutes. 7. Remove and serve with shredded Parmesan on top.

Gold Artichoke Hearts

Prep time: 15 minutes | Cook time: 8 minutes | Serves 4

12 whole artichoke hearts packed in water, drained

60 g plain flour

1 egg

40 g panko bread crumbs

1 teaspoon Italian seasoning

Cooking oil spray

1. Squeeze any excess water from the artichoke hearts and place them on paper towels to dry. 2. Place the flour in a small bowl. 3. In another small bowl, beat the egg. 4. In a third small bowl, stir together the panko and Italian seasoning. 5. Dip the artichoke hearts in the flour, in the egg, and into the panko mixture until coated. 6. Insert the crisper plate into the basket and the basket into the unit. Preheat the unit by selecting AIR FRY, setting the temperature to 192ºC, and setting the time to 3 minutes. Select START/STOP to begin. 7. Once the unit is preheated, spray the crisper plate and the basket with cooking oil. Place the breaded artichoke hearts into the basket, stacking them if needed. 8. Select AIR FRY, set the temperature to 192ºC, and set the time to 8 minutes. Select START/STOP to begin. 9. After 4 minutes, use tongs to flip the artichoke hearts. I recommend flipping instead of shaking because the hearts are small, and this will help keep the breading intact. Re-insert the basket to resume cooking. 10. When the cooking is complete, the artichoke hearts should be deep golden brown and crisp. Cool for 5 minutes before serving.

Roasted Grape Tomatoes and Asparagus

Prep time: 5 minutes | Cook time: 12 minutes | Serves 6

400 g grape tomatoes

1 bunch asparagus, trimmed

2 tablespoons olive oil

3 garlic cloves, minced

½ teaspoon coarse sea salt

1. Preheat the air fryer to 192°C). 2. In a large bowl, combine all of the ingredients, tossing until the vegetables are well coated with oil. 3. Pour the vegetable mixture into the air fryer basket and spread into a single layer, then roast for 12 minutes.

Easy Greek Briami (Ratatouille)

Prep time: 15 minutes | Cook time: 40 minutes | Serves 6

2 Maris Piper potatoes, cubed

100 g plum tomatoes, cubed

1 aubergine, cubed

1 courgette, cubed

1 red onion, chopped

1 red pepper, chopped

2 garlic cloves, minced

1 teaspoon dried mint

1 teaspoon dried parsley

1 teaspoon dried oregano

½ teaspoon salt

½ teaspoon black pepper

¼ teaspoon red pepper flakes

80 ml olive oil

1 (230 g) can tomato paste

65 ml vegetable stock

65 ml water

1. Preheat the air fryer to 160°C. 2. In a large bowl, combine the potatoes, tomatoes, aubergine, courgette onion, bell pepper, garlic, mint, parsley, oregano, salt, black pepper, and red pepper flakes. 3. In a small bowl, mix together the olive oil, tomato paste, stock, and water. 4. Pour the oil-and-tomato-paste mixture over the vegetables and toss until everything is coated. 5. Pour the coated vegetables into the air fryer basket in an even layer and roast for 20 minutes. After 20 minutes, stir well and spread out again. Roast for an additional 10 minutes, then repeat the process and cook for another 10 minutes.

Parmesan-Thyme Butternut Squash

Prep time: 15 minutes | Cook time: 20 minutes | Serves 4

350 g butternut squash, cubed into 1-inch pieces (approximately 1 medium)

2 tablespoons olive oil

¼ teaspoon salt

¼ teaspoon garlic powder

¼ teaspoon black pepper

1 tablespoon fresh thyme

20 g grated Parmesan

1. Preheat the air fryer to 180°C. 2. In a large bowl, combine the cubed squash with the olive oil, salt, garlic powder, pepper, and

thyme until the squash is well coated. 3. Pour this mixture into the air fryer basket, and roast for 10 minutes. Stir and roast another 8 to 10 minutes more. 4. Remove the squash from the air fryer and toss with freshly grated Parmesan before serving.

Crispy Garlic Sliced Aubergine

Prep time: 5 minutes | Cook time: 25 minutes | Serves 4

1 egg

1 tablespoon water

60 g whole wheat bread crumbs

1 teaspoon garlic powder

½ teaspoon dried oregano

½ teaspoon salt

½ teaspoon paprika

1 medium aubergine, sliced into ¼-inch-thick rounds

1 tablespoon olive oil

1. Preheat the air fryer to 180°C. 2. In a medium shallow bowl, beat together the egg and water until frothy. 3. In a separate medium shallow bowl, mix together bread crumbs, garlic powder, oregano, salt, and paprika. 4. Dip each aubergine slice into the egg mixture, then into the bread crumb mixture, coating the outside with crumbs. Place the slices in a single layer in the bottom of the air fryer basket. 5. Drizzle the tops of the aubergine slices with the olive oil, then fry for 15 minutes. Turn each slice and cook for an additional 10 minutes.

Lemony Broccoli

Prep time: 10 minutes | Cook time: 9 to 14 minutes per batch | Serves 4

1 large head broccoli, rinsed and patted dry

2 teaspoons extra-virgin olive oil

1 tablespoon freshly squeezed lemon juice

Olive oil spray

1. Cut off the broccoli florets and separate them. You can use the stems, too; peel the stems and cut them into 1-inch chunks. 2. Insert the crisper plate into the basket and the basket into the unit. Preheat the unit by selecting AIR ROAST, setting the temperature to 200°C, and setting the time to 3 minutes. Select START/STOP to begin. 3. In a large bowl, toss together the broccoli, olive oil, and lemon juice until coated. 4. Once the unit is preheated, spray the crisper plate with olive oil. Working in batches, place half the broccoli into the basket. 5. Select AIR ROAST, set the temperature to 200°C, and set the time to 14 minutes. Select START/STOP to begin. 6. After 5 minutes, remove the basket and shake the broccoli. Reinsert the basket to resume cooking. Check the broccoli after 5 minutes. If it is crisp-tender and slightly brown around the edges, it is done. If not, resume cooking. 7. When the cooking is complete, transfer the broccoli to a serving bowl. Repeat steps 5 and 6 with the remaining broccoli. Serve immediately.

Fried Brussels Sprouts

Prep time: 10 minutes | Cook time: 18 minutes | Serves 4

1 teaspoon plus 1 tablespoon extra-virgin olive oil, divided

2 teaspoons minced garlic

2 tablespoons honey

1 tablespoon sugar

2 tablespoons freshly squeezed lemon juice

2 tablespoons rice vinegar

2 tablespoons sriracha

450 g Brussels sprouts, stems trimmed and any tough leaves removed, rinsed, halved lengthwise, and dried

½ teaspoon salt

Cooking oil spray

1. In a small saucepan over low heat, combine 1 teaspoon of olive oil, the garlic, honey, sugar, lemon juice, vinegar, and sriracha. Cook for 2 to 3 minutes, or until slightly thickened. Remove the pan from the heat, cover, and set aside. 2. Place the Brussels sprouts in a resealable bag or small bowl. Add the remaining olive oil and the salt, and toss to coat. 3. Insert the crisper plate into the basket and the basket into the unit. Preheat the unit by selecting AIR FRY, setting the temperature to 200°C, and setting the time to 3 minutes. Select START/STOP to begin. 4. Once the unit is preheated, spray the crisper plate with cooking oil. Add the Brussels sprouts to the basket. 5. Select AIR FRY, set the temperature to 200°C, and set the time to 15 minutes. Select START/STOP to begin. 6. After 7 or 8 minutes, remove the basket and shake it to toss the sprouts. Reinsert the basket to resume cooking. 7. When the cooking is complete, the leaves should be crispy and light brown and the sprout centres tender. 8. Place the sprouts in a medium serving bowl and drizzle the sauce over the top. Toss to coat, and serve immediately.

Chapter 7 Desserts

Chapter 7 Desserts

Coconut Muffins

Prep time: 5 minutes | Cook time: 25 minutes | Serves 5

55 g coconut flour	1 teaspoon baking powder
2 tablespoons cocoa powder	2 tablespoons coconut oil
3 tablespoons granulated sweetener	2 eggs, beaten
	50 g desiccated coconut

1. In the mixing bowl, mix all ingredients. 2. Then pour the mixture into the molds of the muffin and transfer in the air fryer basket. 3. Cook the muffins at 176ºC for 25 minutes.

Pecan Bars

Prep time: 5 minutes | Cook time: 40 minutes | Serves 12

220 g coconut flour	softened
5 tablespoons granulated sweetener	60 ml heavy cream
4 tablespoons coconut oil,	1 egg, beaten
	4 pecans, chopped

1. Mix coconut flour, sweetener, coconut oil, heavy cream, and egg. 2. Pour the batter in the air fryer basket and flatten well. 3. Top the mixture with pecans and cook the meal at 176ºC for 40 minutes. 4. Cut the cooked meal into the bars.

Mini Peanut Butter Tarts

Prep time: 25 minutes | Cook time: 12 to 15 minutes | Serves 8

125 g pecans	cheese
110 g finely ground blanched almond flour	110 g cream cheese
	140 g sugar-free peanut butter
2 tablespoons unsalted butter, at room temperature	1 teaspoon pure vanilla extract
	⅛ teaspoon sea salt
50 g powdered sweetener, plus	85 g organic chocolate chips
2 tablespoons, divided	1 tablespoon coconut oil
120 g heavy (whipping) cream	40 g chopped peanuts or pecans
2 tablespoons mascarpone	

1. Place the pecans in the bowl of a food processor; process until they are finely ground. 2. Transfer the ground pecans to a medium bowl and stir in the almond flour. Add the butter and 2 tablespoons of sweetener and stir until the mixture becomes wet and crumbly.

3. Divide the mixture among 8 silicone muffin cups, pressing the crust firmly with your fingers into the bottom and part way up the sides of each cup. 4. Arrange the muffin cups in the air fryer basket, working in batches if necessary. Set the air fryer to 148ºC and bake for 12 to 15 minutes, until the crusts begin to brown. Remove the cups from the air fryer and set them aside to cool. 5. In the bowl of a stand mixer, combine the heavy cream and mascarpone cheese. Beat until peaks form. Transfer to a large bowl. 6. In the same stand mixer bowl, combine the cream cheese, peanut butter, remaining 50 g sweetener, vanilla, and salt. Beat at medium-high speed until smooth. 7. Reduce the speed to low and add the heavy cream mixture back a spoonful at a time, beating after each addition. 8. Spoon the peanut butter mixture over the crusts and freeze the tarts for 30 minutes. 9. Place the chocolate chips and coconut oil in the top of a double boiler over high heat. Stir until melted, then remove from the heat. 10. Drizzle the melted chocolate over the peanut butter tarts. Top with the chopped nuts and freeze the tarts for another 15 minutes, until set. 11. Store the peanut butter tarts in an airtight container in the refrigerator for up to 1 week or in the freezer for up to 1 month.

New York Cheesecake

Prep time: 1 hour | Cook time: 37 minutes | Serves 8

170 g almond flour	340 g granulated sweetener
85 g powdered sweetener	3 eggs, at room temperature
55 g unsalted butter, melted	1 tablespoon vanilla essence
565 g full-fat cream cheese	1 teaspoon grated lemon zest
120 ml heavy cream	

1. Coat the sides and bottom of a baking pan with a little flour. 2. In a mixing bowl, combine the almond flour and powdered sweetener. Add the melted butter and mix until your mixture looks like breadcrumbs. 3. Press the mixture into the bottom of the prepared pan to form an even layer. Bake at 164ºC for 7 minutes until golden brown. Allow it to cool completely on a wire rack. 4. Meanwhile, in a mixer fitted with the paddle attachment, prepare the filling by mixing the soft cheese, heavy cream, and granulated sweetener; beat until creamy and fluffy. 5. Crack the eggs into the mixing bowl, one at a time; add the vanilla and lemon zest and continue to mix until fully combined. 6. Pour the prepared topping over the cooled crust and spread evenly. 7. Bake in the preheated air fryer at 164ºC for 25 to 30 minutes; leave it in the air fryer to keep warm for another 30 minutes. 8. Cover your cheesecake with plastic wrap. Place in your refrigerator and allow it to cool at least 6 hours or overnight. Serve well chilled.

Vanilla Scones

Prep time: 20 minutes | Cook time: 10 minutes | Serves 6

110 g coconut flour
½ teaspoon baking powder
1 teaspoon apple cider vinegar
2 teaspoons mascarpone
60 ml heavy cream
1 teaspoon vanilla extract
1 tablespoon granulated sweetener
Cooking spray

1. In the mixing bowl, mix coconut flour with baking powder, apple cider vinegar, mascarpone, heavy cream, vanilla extract, and sweetener. 2. Knead the dough and cut into scones. 3. Then put them in the air fryer basket and sprinkle with cooking spray. 4. Cook the vanilla scones at 185°C for 10 minutes.

Homemade Mint Pie

Prep time: 15 minutes | Cook time: 25 minutes | Serves 2

1 tablespoon instant coffee
2 tablespoons almond butter, softened
2 tablespoons granulated sweetener
1 teaspoon dried mint
3 eggs, beaten
1 teaspoon dried spearmint
4 teaspoons coconut flour
Cooking spray

1. Spray the air fryer basket with cooking spray. 2. Then mix all ingredients in the mixer bowl. 3. When you get a smooth mixture, transfer it in the air fryer basket. Flatten it gently. Cook the pie at 185°C for 25 minutes.

Strawberry Pecan Pie

Prep time: 15 minutes | Cook time: 10 minutes | Serves 6

190 g whole shelled pecans
1 tablespoon unsalted butter, softened
240 ml heavy whipping cream
12 medium fresh strawberries, hulled
2 tablespoons sour cream

1. Place pecans and butter into a food processor and pulse ten times until a dough forms. Press dough into the bottom of an ungreased round nonstick baking dish. 2. Place dish into air fryer basket. Adjust the temperature to 160°C and set the timer for 10 minutes. Crust will be firm and golden when done. Let cool 20 minutes. 3. In a large bowl, whisk cream until fluffy and doubled in size, about 2 minutes. 4. In a separate large bowl, mash strawberries until mostly liquid. Fold strawberries and sour cream into whipped cream. 5. Spoon mixture into cooled crust, cover, and place in refrigerator for at least 30 minutes to set. Serve chilled.

Zucchini Bread

Prep time: 10 minutes | Cook time: 40 minutes | Serves 12

220 g coconut flour
2 teaspoons baking powder
150 g granulated sweetener
120 ml coconut oil, melted
1 teaspoon apple cider vinegar
1 teaspoon vanilla extract
3 eggs, beaten
1 courgette, grated
1 teaspoon ground cinnamon

1. In the mixing bowl, mix coconut flour with baking powder, sweetener, coconut oil, apple cider vinegar, vanilla extract, eggs, courgette, and ground cinnamon. 2. Transfer the mixture into the air fryer basket and flatten it in the shape of the bread. 3. Cook the bread at 176°C for 40 minutes.

Chocolate Chip Cookie Cake

Prep time: 5 minutes | Cook time: 15 minutes | Serves 8

4 tablespoons salted butter, melted
65 g granular brown sweetener
1 large egg
½ teaspoon vanilla extract
110 g blanched finely ground almond flour
½ teaspoon baking powder
40 g low-carb chocolate chips

1. In a large bowl, whisk together butter, sweetener, egg, and vanilla. Add flour and baking powder and stir until combined. 2. Fold in chocolate chips, then spoon batter into an ungreased round nonstick baking dish. 3. Place dish into air fryer basket. Adjust the temperature to 148°C and set the timer for 15 minutes. When edges are browned, cookie cake will be done. 4. Slice and serve warm.

Honeyed, Roasted Apples with Walnuts

Prep time: 5 minutes | Cook time: 12 to 15 minutes | Serves 4

2 Granny Smith apples
20 g certified gluten-free rolled oats
2 tablespoons honey
½ teaspoon ground cinnamon
2 tablespoons chopped walnuts
Pinch salt
1 tablespoon olive oil

1. Preheat the air fryer to 192°C. 2. Core the apples and slice them in half. 3. In a medium bowl, mix together the oats, honey, cinnamon, walnuts, salt, and olive oil. 4. Scoop a quarter of the oat mixture onto the top of each half apple. 5. Place the apples in the air fryer basket, and roast for 12 to 15 minutes, or until the apples are fork tender.

Roasted Honey Pears

Prep time: 7 minutes | Cook time: 18 to 23 minutes | Serves 4

2 large Bosc pears, halved lengthwise and seeded
3 tablespoons honey
1 tablespoon unsalted butter
½ teaspoon ground cinnamon
30 g walnuts, chopped
55 g part-skim ricotta cheese, divided

1. Insert the crisper plate into the basket and the basket into the unit. Preheat to 176°C. 2. In a 6-by-2-inch round pan, place the pears cut-side up. 3. In a small microwave-safe bowl, melt the honey, butter, and cinnamon. Brush this mixture over the cut sides of the pears. Pour 3 tablespoons of water around the pears in the pan. 4. Once the unit is preheated, place the pan into the basket. 5. After about 18 minutes, check the pears. They should be tender when pierced with a fork and slightly crisp on the edges. If not, resume cooking. 6. When the cooking is complete, baste the pears once with the liquid in the pan. Carefully remove the pears from the pan and place on a serving plate. Drizzle each with some liquid from the pan, sprinkle the walnuts on top, and serve with a spoonful of ricotta cheese.

Lemon Bars

Prep time: 15 minutes | Cook time: 25 minutes | Serves 6

90 g whole-wheat pastry flour
2 tablespoons icing sugar
55 g unsalted butter, melted
100 g granulated sugar
1 tablespoon packed grated lemon zest
60 ml freshly squeezed lemon juice
⅛ teaspoon sea salt
60 g unsweetened plain applesauce
2 teaspoons cornflour
¾ teaspoon baking powder
Cooking oil spray (sunflower, safflower, or refined coconut)

1. In a small bowl, stir together the flour, icing sugar, and melted butter just until well combined. Place in the refrigerator. 2. In a medium bowl, stir together the granulated sugar, lemon zest and juice, salt, applesauce, cornflour, and baking powder. 3. Insert the crisper plate into the basket and the basket into the unit. Preheat to 176°C. 4. Spray a 6-by-2-inch round pan lightly with cooking oil. Remove the crust mixture from the refrigerator and gently press it into the bottom of the prepared pan in an even layer. 5. Once the unit is preheated, place the pan into the basket. 6. Cook for 5 minutes, then check the crust. It should be slightly firm to the touch. Remove the pan and spread the lemon filling over the crust. Reinsert the pan into the basket and resume baking for 18 to 20 minutes, or until the top is nicely browned. 7. When baking is complete, let cool for 30 minutes. Refrigerate to cool completely. Cut into pieces and serve.

Biscuit-Base Cheesecake

Prep time: 10 minutes | Cook time: 20 minutes | Serves 8

100 g crushed digestive biscuits
3 tablespoons butter, at room temperature
225 g cream cheese, at room temperature
65 g granulated sugar
2 eggs, beaten
1 tablespoon all-purpose flour
1 teaspoon vanilla extract
60 ml chocolate syrup

1. In a small bowl, stir together the crushed biscuits and butter. Press the crust into the bottom of a 6-by-2-inch round baking pan and freeze to set while you prepare the filling. 2. In a medium bowl, stir together the cream cheese and sugar until mixed well. 3. One at a time, beat in the eggs. Add the flour and vanilla and stir to combine. 4. Transfer ⅓ of the filling to a small bowl and stir in the chocolate syrup until combined. 5. Insert the crisper plate into the basket and the basket into the unit. Preheat the air fryer to 164°C, and bake for 3 minutes. 6. Pour the vanilla filling into the pan with the crust. Drop the chocolate filling over the vanilla filling by the spoonful. With a clean butter knife stir the fillings in a zigzag pattern to marble them. Do not let the knife touch the crust. 7. Once the unit is preheated, place the pan into the basket. 8. Set the temperature to 164°C, and bake for 20 minutes. 9. When the cooking is done, the cheesecake should be just set. Cool on a wire rack for 1 hour. Refrigerate the cheesecake until firm before slicing.

Hazelnut Butter Cookies

Prep time: 30 minutes | Cook time: 20 minutes | Serves 10

4 tablespoons liquid monk fruit, or agave syrup
65 g hazelnuts, ground
110 g unsalted butter, room temperature
190 g almond flour
110 g coconut flour
55 g granulated sweetener
2 teaspoons ground cinnamon

1. Firstly, cream liquid monk fruit with butter until the mixture becomes fluffy. Sift in both types of flour. 2. Now, stir in the hazelnuts. Now, knead the mixture to form a dough; place in the refrigerator for about 35 minutes. 3. To finish, shape the prepared dough into the bite-sized balls; arrange them on a baking dish; flatten the balls using the back of a spoon. 4. Mix granulated sweetener with ground cinnamon. Press your cookies in the cinnamon mixture until they are completely covered. 5. Bake the cookies for 20 minutes at 154°C. 6. Leave them to cool for about 10 minutes before transferring them to a wire rack. Bon appétit!

Cherry Pie

Prep time: 15 minutes | Cook time: 35 minutes | Serves 6

Plain flour, for dusting	1 egg
1 package of shortcrust pastry, cut in half, at room temperature	1 tablespoon water
350 g can cherry pie filling	1 tablespoon sugar

1. Dust a work surface with flour and place the piecrust on it. Roll out the piecrust. Invert a shallow air fryer baking pan, or your own pie pan that fits inside the air fryer basket, on top of the dough. Trim the dough around the pan, making your cut ½ inch wider than the pan itself. 2. Repeat with the second piecrust but make the cut the same size as or slightly smaller than the pan. 3. Put the larger crust in the bottom of the baking pan. Don't stretch the dough. Gently press it into the pan. 4. Spoon in enough cherry pie filling to fill the crust. Do not overfill. 5. Using a knife or pizza cutter, cut the second piecrust into 1-inch-wide strips. Weave the strips in a lattice pattern over the top of the cherry pie filling. 6. Insert the crisper plate into the basket and the basket into the unit. Preheat to 164°C. 7. In a small bowl, whisk the egg and water. Gently brush the egg wash over the top of the pie. Sprinkle with the sugar and cover the pie with aluminum foil. 8. Once the unit is preheated, place the pie into the basket. 9. Bake for 30 minutes, remove the foil and resume cooking for 3 to 5 minutes more. The finished pie should have a flaky golden-brown crust and bubbling pie filling. 10. When the cooking is complete, serve warm. Refrigerate leftovers for a few days.

Rhubarb and Strawberry Crumble

Prep time: 10 minutes | Cook time: 12 to 17 minutes | Serves 6

250 g sliced fresh strawberries	or plain flour
95 g sliced rhubarb	50 g packed light brown sugar
75 g granulated sugar	½ teaspoon ground cinnamon
60 g quick-cooking oatmeal	3 tablespoons unsalted butter, melted
50 g whole-wheat pastry flour,	

1. Insert the crisper plate into the basket and the basket into the unit. Preheat the unit to 192°C. 2. In a 6-by-2-inch round metal baking pan, combine the strawberries, rhubarb, and granulated sugar. 3. In a medium bowl, stir together the oatmeal, flour, brown sugar, and cinnamon. Stir the melted butter into this mixture until crumbly. Sprinkle the crumble mixture over the fruit. 4. Once the unit is preheated, place the pan into the basket. 5.Bake for 12 minutes then check the crumble. If the fruit is bubbling and the topping is golden brown, it is done. If not, resume cooking. 6. When the cooking is complete, serve warm.

Pineapple Wontons

Prep time: 15 minutes | Cook time: 15 to 18 minutes per batch | Serves 5

225 g cream cheese	20 wonton wrappers
170 g finely chopped fresh pineapple	Cooking oil spray

1. In a small microwave-safe bowl, heat the cream cheese in the microwave on high power for 20 seconds to soften. 2. In a medium bowl, stir together the cream cheese and pineapple until mixed well. 3. Lay out the wonton wrappers on a work surface. A clean table or large cutting board works well. 4. Spoon 1½ teaspoons of the cream cheese mixture onto each wrapper. Be careful not to overfill. 5. Fold each wrapper diagonally across to form a triangle. Bring the 2 bottom corners up toward each other. Do not close the wrapper yet. Bring up the 2 open sides and push out any air. Squeeze the open edges together to seal. 6. Insert the crisper plate into the basket and the basket into the unit. Preheat the air fryer to 200°C. 7. Once the unit is preheated, spray the crisper plate with cooking oil. Place the wontons into the basket. You can work in batches or stack the wontons. Spray the wontons with the cooking oil. 8. Cook wontons for 10 minutes, then remove the basket, flip each wonton, and spray them with more oil. Reinsert the basket to resume cooking for 5 to 8 minutes more until the wontons are light golden brown and crisp. 9. If cooking in batches, remove the cooked wontons from the basket and repeat steps 7 and 8 for the remaining wontons. 10. When the cooking is complete, cool for 5 minutes before serving.

Pecan Butter Cookies

Prep time: 5 minutes | Cook time: 24 minutes | Makes 12 cookies

125 g chopped pecans	150 g granulated sweetener, divided
110 g salted butter, melted	
55 g coconut flour	1 teaspoon vanilla extract

1. In a food processor, blend together pecans, butter, flour, 100 g sweetener, and vanilla 1 minute until a dough forms. 2. Form dough into twelve individual cookie balls, about 1 tablespoon each. 3. Cut three pieces of baking paper to fit air fryer basket. Place four cookies on each ungreased baking paper and place one piece baking paper with cookies into air fryer basket. Adjust air fryer temperature to 164°C and set the timer for 8 minutes. Repeat cooking with remaining batches. 4. When the timer goes off, allow cookies to cool 5 minutes on a large serving plate until cool enough to handle. While still warm, dust cookies with remaining granulated sweetener. Allow to cool completely, about 15 minutes, before serving.

Vanilla Cookies with Hazelnuts

Prep time: 20 minutes | Cook time: 10 minutes | Serves 6

110 g almond flour	120 g powdered sweetener
55 g coconut flour	2 teaspoons vanilla
1 teaspoon baking soda	2 eggs, at room temperature
1 teaspoon fine sea salt	130 g hazelnuts, coarsely
110 g unsalted butter	chopped

1.Preheat the air fryer to 176°C. 2. Mix the flour with the baking soda, and sea salt. 3. In the bowl of an electric mixer, beat the butter, sweetener, and vanilla until creamy. Fold in the eggs, one at a time, and mix until well combined. 4. Slowly and gradually, stir in the flour mixture. Finally, fold in the coarsely chopped hazelnuts. 5. Divide the dough into small balls using a large cookie scoop; drop onto the prepared cookie sheets. Bake for 10 minutes or until golden brown, rotating the pan once or twice through the cooking time. 6. Work in batches and cool for a couple of minutes before removing to wire racks. Enjoy!

Baked Apples and Walnuts

Prep time: 6 minutes | Cook time: 20 minutes | Serves 4

4 small Granny Smith apples	1 teaspoon ground cinnamon
50 g chopped walnuts	½ teaspoon ground nutmeg
50 g light brown sugar	120 ml water, or apple juice
2 tablespoons butter, melted	

1. Cut off the top third of the apples. Spoon out the core and some of the flesh and discard. Place the apples in a small air fryer baking pan. 2. Insert the crisper plate into the basket and the basket into the unit. Preheat to 176°C. 3. In a small bowl, stir together the walnuts, brown sugar, melted butter, cinnamon, and nutmeg. Spoon this mixture into the centers of the hollowed-out apples. 4. Once the unit is preheated, pour the water into the crisper plate. Place the baking pan into the basket. 5. Bake for 20 minutes. 6. When the cooking is complete, the apples should be bubbly and fork tender.

Simple Apple Turnovers

Prep time: 10 minutes | Cook time: 10 minutes | Serves 4

1 apple, peeled, quartered, and thinly sliced	1 tablespoon granulated sugar
½ teaspoons pumpkin pie spice	Pinch of kosher, or coarse sea salt
Juice of ½ lemon	6 sheets filo pastry

1. Preheat the air fryer to 164°C. 2. In a medium bowl, combine the apple, pumpkin pie spice, lemon juice, granulated sugar, and kosher salt. 3. Cut the filo pastry sheets into 4 equal pieces and place individual tablespoons of apple filling in the center of each piece, then fold in both sides and roll from front to back. 4. Spray the air fryer basket with nonstick cooking spray, then place the turnovers in the basket and bake for 10 minutes or until golden brown. 5. Remove the turnovers from the air fryer and allow to cool on a wire rack for 10 minutes before serving.

Dark Chocolate Lava Cake

Prep time: 5 minutes | Cook time: 10 minutes | Serves 4

Olive oil cooking spray	½ teaspoon baking powder
30 g whole wheat flour	60 ml raw honey
1 tablespoon unsweetened dark chocolate cocoa powder	1 egg
⅛ teaspoon salt	2 tablespoons olive oil

1. Preheat the air fryer to 192°C. Lightly coat the insides of four ramekins with olive oil cooking spray. 2. In a medium bowl, combine the flour, cocoa powder, salt, baking powder, honey, egg, and olive oil. 3. Divide the batter evenly among the ramekins. 4. Place the filled ramekins inside the air fryer and bake for 10 minutes. 5. Remove the lava cakes from the air fryer and slide a knife around the outside edge of each cake. Turn each ramekin upside down on a saucer and serve.

Pretzels

Prep time: 10 minutes | Cook time: 10 minutes | Serves 6

335 g shredded Mozzarella cheese	2 tablespoons salted butter, melted, divided
110 g blanched finely ground almond flour	50 g granular sweetener, divided
	1 teaspoon ground cinnamon

1. Place Mozzarella, flour, 1 tablespoon butter, and 2 tablespoons sweetener in a large microwave-safe bowl. Microwave on high 45 seconds, then stir with a fork until a smooth dough ball forms. 2. Separate dough into six equal sections. Gently roll each section into a 12-inch rope, then fold into a pretzel shape. 3. Place pretzels into ungreased air fryer basket. Adjust the temperature to 188°C and set the timer for 8 minutes, turning pretzels halfway through cooking. 4. In a small bowl, combine remaining butter, remaining sweetener, and cinnamon. Brush ½ mixture on both sides of pretzels. 5. Place pretzels back into air fryer and cook an additional 2 minutes. 6. Transfer pretzels to a large plate. Brush on both sides with remaining butter mixture, then let cool 5 minutes before serving.

Butter and Chocolate Chip Cookies

Prep time: 20 minutes | Cook time: 11 minutes | Serves 8

110 g unsalted butter, at room temperature
155 g powdered sweetener
60 g chunky peanut butter
1 teaspoon vanilla paste
1 fine almond flour
75 g coconut flour

35 g cocoa powder, unsweetened
1 ½ teaspoons baking powder
¼ teaspoon ground cinnamon
¼ teaspoon ginger
85 g unsweetened, or dark chocolate chips

1. In a mixing dish, beat the butter and sweetener until creamy and uniform. Stir in the peanut butter and vanilla. 2. In another mixing dish, thoroughly combine the flour, cocoa powder, baking powder, cinnamon, and ginger. 3. Add the flour mixture to the peanut butter mixture; mix to combine well. Afterwards, fold in the chocolate chips. Drop by large spoonsful onto a baking paper-lined air fryer basket. Bake at 185°C for 11 minutes or until golden brown on the top. Bon appétit!

Baked Cheesecake

Prep time: 30 minutes | Cook time: 35 minutes | Serves 6

50 g almond flour
1½ tablespoons unsalted butter, melted
2 tablespoons granulated sweetener
225 g cream cheese, softened
25 g powdered sweetener
½ teaspoon vanilla paste

1 egg, at room temperature
Topping:
355 ml sour cream
3 tablespoons powdered sweetener
1 teaspoon vanilla extract

1. Thoroughly combine the almond flour, butter, and 2 tablespoons of granulated sweetener in a mixing bowl. Press the mixture into the bottom of lightly greased custard cups. 2. Then, mix the cream cheese, 25 g of powdered sweetener, vanilla, and egg using an electric mixer on low speed. Pour the batter into the pan, covering the crust. 3. Bake in the preheated air fryer at 164°C for 35 minutes until edges are puffed and the surface is firm. 4. Mix the sour cream, 3 tablespoons of powdered sweetener, and vanilla for the topping; spread over the crust and allow it to cool to room temperature. 5. Transfer to your refrigerator for 6 to 8 hours. Serve well chilled.

Butter Flax Cookies

Prep time: 25 minutes | Cook time: 20 minutes | Serves 4

225 g almond meal
2 tablespoons flaxseed meal
30 g monk fruit, or equivalent sweetener
1 teaspoon baking powder
A pinch of grated nutmeg

A pinch of coarse salt
1 large egg, room temperature.
110 g unsalted butter, room temperature
1 teaspoon vanilla extract

1. Mix the almond meal, flaxseed meal, monk fruit, baking powder, grated nutmeg, and salt in a bowl. 2. In a separate bowl, whisk the egg, butter, and vanilla extract. 3. Stir the egg mixture into dry mixture; mix to combine well or until it forms a nice, soft dough. 4. Roll your dough out and cut out with a cookie cutter of your choice. Bake in the preheated air fryer at 176°C for 10 minutes. Decrease the temperature to 164°C and cook for 10 minutes longer. Bon appétit!

Chapter 8 Snacks and Appetizers

Chapter 8 Snacks and Appetizers

Baked Ricotta

Prep time: 10 minutes | Cook time: 15 minutes | Makes 475 ml

1 (425 g) container whole milk Ricotta cheese
3 tablespoons grated Parmesan cheese, divided
2 tablespoons extra-virgin olive oil
1 teaspoon chopped fresh thyme leaves
1 teaspoon grated lemon zest
1 clove garlic, crushed with press
¼ teaspoon salt
¼ teaspoon pepper
Toasted baguette slices or crackers, for serving

1. Preheat the air fryer to 192ºC. 2. To get the baking dish in and out of the air fryer, create a sling using a 24-inch length of foil, folded lengthwise into thirds. 3. Whisk together the Ricotta, 2 tablespoons of the Parmesan, oil, thyme, lemon zest, garlic, salt, and pepper. Pour into a baking dish. Cover the dish tightly with foil. 4. Place the sling under dish and lift by the ends into the air fryer, tucking the ends of the sling around the dish. Bake for 10 minutes. Remove the foil cover and sprinkle with the remaining 1 tablespoon of the Parmesan. Air fry for 5 more minutes, or until bubbly at edges and the top is browned. 5. Serve warm with toasted baguette slices or crackers.

Lemony Pear Chips

Prep time: 15 minutes | Cook time: 9 to 13 minutes | Serves 4

2 firm Bosc or Anjou pears, cut crosswise into ⅛-inch-thick slices
1 tablespoon freshly squeezed lemon juice
½ teaspoon ground cinnamon
⅛ teaspoon ground cardamom

1. Preheat the air fryer to 192ºC. 2. Separate the smaller stem-end pear rounds from the larger rounds with seeds. Remove the core and seeds from the larger slices. Sprinkle all slices with lemon juice, cinnamon, and cardamom. 3. Put the smaller chips into the air fryer basket. Air fry for 3 to 5 minutes, or until light golden brown, shaking the basket once during cooking. Remove from the air fryer. 4. Repeat with the larger slices, air frying for 6 to 8 minutes, or until light golden brown, shaking the basket once during cooking. 5. Remove the chips from the air fryer. Cool and serve or store in an airtight container at room temperature up for to 2 days.

Bacon-Wrapped Shrimp and Jalapeño

Prep time: 20 minutes | Cook time: 26 minutes | Serves 8

24 large shrimp, peeled and deveined, about 340 g
5 tablespoons barbecue sauce,
divided
12 strips bacon, cut in half
24 small pickled jalapeño slices

1. Toss together the shrimp and 3 tablespoons of the barbecue sauce. Let stand for 15 minutes. Soak 24 wooden toothpicks in water for 10 minutes. Wrap 1 piece bacon around the shrimp and jalapeño slice, then secure with a toothpick. 2. Preheat the air fryer to 176ºC. 3. Working in batches, place half of the shrimp in the air fryer basket, spacing them ½ inch apart. Air fry for 10 minutes. Turn shrimp over with tongs and air fry for 3 minutes more, or until bacon is golden brown and shrimp are cooked through. 4. Brush with the remaining barbecue sauce and serve.

Garlicky and Cheesy French Fries

Prep time: 5 minutes | Cook time: 20 to 25 minutes | Serves 4

3 medium russet or Maris Piper potatoes, rinsed, dried, and cut into thin wedges or classic fry shapes
2 tablespoons extra-virgin olive oil
1 tablespoon granulated garlic
80 ml grated Parmesan cheese
½ teaspoon salt
¼ teaspoon freshly ground black pepper
Cooking oil spray
2 tablespoons finely chopped fresh parsley (optional)

1. In a large bowl combine the potato wedges or fries and the olive oil. Toss to coat. 2. Sprinkle the potatoes with the granulated garlic, Parmesan cheese, salt, and pepper, and toss again. 3. Insert the crisper plate into the basket and the basket into the unit. Preheat the unit by selecting AIR FRY, setting the temperature to 204ºC, and setting the time to 3 minutes. Select START/STOP to begin. 4. Once the unit is preheated, spray the crisper plate with cooking oil. Place the potatoes into the basket. 5. Select AIR FRY, set the temperature to 204ºC, and set the time to 20 to 25 minutes. Select START/STOP to begin. 6. After about 10 minutes, remove the basket and shake it so the fries at the bottom come up to the top. Reinsert the basket to resume cooking. 7. When the cooking is complete, top the fries with the parsley (if using) and serve hot.

Classic Spring Rolls

Prep time: 10 minutes | Cook time: 9 minutes | Makes 16 spring rolls

4 teaspoons toasted sesame oil

6 medium garlic cloves, minced or pressed

1 tablespoon grated peeled fresh ginger

475 ml thinly sliced shiitake mushrooms

1 L chopped green cabbage

240 ml grated carrot

½ teaspoon sea salt

16 rice paper wrappers

Cooking oil spray (sunflower, safflower, or refined coconut)

Gluten-free sweet and sour sauce or Thai sweet chilli sauce, for serving (optional)

1. Place a wok or sauté pan over medium heat until hot. 2. Add the sesame oil, garlic, ginger, mushrooms, cabbage, carrot, and salt. Cook for 3 to 4 minutes, stirring often, until the cabbage is lightly wilted. Remove the pan from the heat. 3. Gently run a rice paper under water. Lay it on a flat non-absorbent surface. Place about 60 ml of the cabbage filling in the middle. Once the wrapper is soft enough to roll, fold the bottom up over the filling, fold in the sides, and roll the wrapper all the way up. (Basically, make a tiny burrito.) 4. Repeat step 3 to make the remaining spring rolls until you have the number of spring rolls you want to cook right now (and the amount that will fit in the air fryer basket in a single layer without them touching each other). Refrigerate any leftover filling in an airtight container for about 1 week. 5. Insert the crisper plate into the basket and the basket into the unit. Preheat the unit by selecting AIR FRY, setting the temperature to 200°C, and setting the time to 3 minutes. Select START/STOP to begin. 6. Once the unit is preheated, spray the crisper plate and the basket with cooking oil. Place the spring rolls into the basket, leaving a little room between them so they don't stick to each other. Spray the top of each spring roll with cooking oil. 7. Select AIR FRY, set the temperature to 200°C, and set the time to 9 minutes. Select START/STOP to begin. 8. When the cooking is complete, the egg rolls should be crisp-ish and lightly browned. Serve immediately, plain or with a sauce of choice.

Shishito Peppers with Herb Dressing

Prep time: 10 minutes | Cook time: 6 minutes | Serves 2 to 4

170 g shishito or Padron peppers

1 tablespoon vegetable oil

Rock salt and freshly ground black pepper, to taste

120 ml mayonnaise

2 tablespoons finely chopped fresh basil leaves

2 tablespoons finely chopped

fresh flat-leaf parsley

1 tablespoon finely chopped fresh tarragon

1 tablespoon finely chopped fresh chives

Finely grated zest of ½ lemon

1 tablespoon fresh lemon juice

Flaky sea salt, for serving

1. Preheat the air fryer to 204°C. 2. In a bowl, toss together the shishitos and oil to evenly coat and season with rock salt and black pepper. Transfer to the air fryer and air fry for 6 minutes, shaking the basket halfway through, or until the shishitos are blistered and lightly charred. 3. Meanwhile, in a small bowl, whisk together the mayonnaise, basil, parsley, tarragon, chives, lemon zest, and lemon juice. 4. Pile the peppers on a plate, sprinkle with flaky sea salt, and serve hot with the dressing.

Rosemary-Garlic Shoestring Fries

Prep time: 5 minutes | Cook time: 18 minutes | Serves 2

1 large russet or Maris Piper potato (about 340 g), scrubbed clean, and julienned

1 tablespoon vegetable oil

Leaves from 1 sprig fresh

rosemary

Rock salt and freshly ground black pepper, to taste

1 garlic clove, thinly sliced

Flaky sea salt, for serving

1. Preheat the air fryer to 204°C. 2. Place the julienned potatoes in a large colander and rinse under cold running water until the water runs clear. Spread the potatoes out on a double-thick layer of paper towels and pat dry. 3. In a large bowl, combine the potatoes, oil, and rosemary. Season with rock salt and pepper and toss to coat evenly. Place the potatoes in the air fryer and air fry for 18 minutes, shaking the basket every 5 minutes and adding the garlic in the last 5 minutes of cooking, or until the fries are golden brown and crisp. 4. Transfer the fries to a plate and sprinkle with flaky sea salt while they're hot. Serve immediately.

Peppery Chicken Meatballs

Prep time: 5 minutes | Cook time: 13 to 20 minutes | Makes 16 meatballs

2 teaspoons olive oil

60 ml minced onion

60 ml minced red pepper

2 vanilla wafers, crushed

1 egg white

½ teaspoon dried thyme

230 g minced chicken breast

1. Preheat the air fryer to 188°C. 2. In a baking pan, mix the olive oil, onion, and red pepper. Put the pan in the air fryer. Air fry for 3 to 5 minutes, or until the vegetables are tender. 3. In a medium bowl, mix the cooked vegetables, crushed wafers, egg white, and thyme until well combined 4. Mix in the chicken, gently but thoroughly, until everything is combined. 5. Form the mixture into 16 meatballs and place them in the air fryer basket. Air fry for 10 to 15 minutes, or until the meatballs reach an internal temperature of 74°C on a meat thermometer. 6. Serve immediately.

Veggie Shrimp Toast

Prep time: 15 minutes | Cook time: 3 to 6 minutes | Serves 4

8 large raw shrimp, peeled and finely chopped

1 egg white

2 garlic cloves, minced

3 tablespoons minced red pepper

1 medium celery stalk, minced

2 tablespoons cornflour

¼ teaspoon Chinese five-spice powder

3 slices firm thin-sliced no-salt wholemeal bread

1. Preheat the air fryer to 176ºC. 2. In a small bowl, stir together the shrimp, egg white, garlic, red pepper, celery, cornflour, and five-spice powder. Top each slice of bread with one-third of the shrimp mixture, spreading it evenly to the edges. With a sharp knife, cut each slice of bread into 4 strips. 3. Place the shrimp toasts in the air fryer basket in a single layer. You may need to cook them in batches. Air fry for 3 to 6 minutes, until crisp and golden brown. 4. Serve hot.

Veggie Salmon Nachos

Prep time: 10 minutes | Cook time: 9 to 12 minutes | Serves 6

57 g baked no-salt corn tortilla chips

1 (142 g) baked salmon fillet, flaked

120 ml canned low-salt black beans, rinsed and drained

1 red pepper, chopped

120 ml grated carrot

1 jalapeño pepper, minced

80 ml shredded low-salt low-fat Swiss cheese

1 tomato, chopped

1. Preheat the air fryer to 182ºC. 2. In a baking pan, layer the tortilla chips. Top with the salmon, black beans, red pepper, carrot, jalapeño, and Swiss cheese. 3. Bake in the air fryer for 9 to 12 minutes, or until the cheese is melted and starts to brown. 4. Top with the tomato and serve.

Air Fried Pot Stickers

Prep time: 10 minutes | Cook time: 18 to 20 minutes | Makes 30 pot stickers

120 ml finely chopped cabbage

60 ml finely chopped red pepper

2 spring onions, finely chopped

1 egg, beaten

2 tablespoons cocktail sauce

2 teaspoons low-salt soy sauce

30 wonton wrappers

1 tablespoon water, for brushing the wrappers

1. Preheat the air fryer to 182ºC. 2. In a small bowl, combine the cabbage, pepper, spring onions, egg, cocktail sauce, and soy sauce, and mix well. 3. Put about 1 teaspoon of the mixture in the centre of each wonton wrapper. Fold the wrapper in half, covering the filling; dampen the edges with water, and seal. You can crimp the edges of the wrapper with your fingers, so they look like the pot stickers you get in restaurants. Brush them with water. 4. Place the pot stickers in the air fryer basket and air fry in 2 batches for 9 to 10 minutes, or until the pot stickers are hot and the bottoms are lightly browned. 5. Serve hot.

Beef and Mango Skewers

Prep time: 10 minutes | Cook time: 4 to 7 minutes | Serves 4

340 g beef sirloin tip, cut into 1-inch cubes

2 tablespoons balsamic vinegar

1 tablespoon olive oil

1 tablespoon honey

½ teaspoon dried marjoram

Pinch of salt

Freshly ground black pepper, to taste

1 mango

1. Preheat the air fryer to 200ºC. 2. Put the beef cubes in a medium bowl and add the balsamic vinegar, olive oil, honey, marjoram, salt, and pepper. Mix well, then massage the marinade into the beef with your hands. Set aside. 3. To prepare the mango, stand it on end and cut the skin off, using a sharp knife. Then carefully cut around the oval pit to remove the flesh. Cut the mango into 1-inch cubes. 4. Thread metal skewers alternating with three beef cubes and two mango cubes. 5. Roast the skewers in the air fryer basket for 4 to 7 minutes, or until the beef is browned and at least 63ºC. 6. Serve hot.

Crispy Filo Artichoke Triangles

Prep time: 15 minutes | Cook time: 9 to 12 minutes | Makes 18 triangles

60 ml Ricotta cheese

1 egg white

80 ml minced and drained artichoke hearts

3 tablespoons grated Mozzarella

cheese

½ teaspoon dried thyme

6 sheets frozen filo pastry, thawed

2 tablespoons melted butter

1. Preheat the air fryer to 204ºC. 2. In a small bowl, combine the Ricotta cheese, egg white, artichoke hearts, Mozzarella cheese, and thyme, and mix well. 3. Cover the filo pastry with a damp kitchen towel while you work so it doesn't dry out. Using one sheet at a time, place on the work surface and cut into thirds lengthwise. 4. Put about 1½ teaspoons of the filling on each strip at the base. Fold the bottom right-hand tip of phyllo over the filling to meet the other side in a triangle, then continue folding in a triangle. Brush each triangle with butter to seal the edges. Repeat with the remaining phyllo dough and filling. 5. Place the triangles in the air fryer basket. Bake, 6 at a time, for about 3 to 4 minutes, or until the filo is golden brown and crisp. 6. Serve hot.

Sweet Bacon Potato Crunchies

Prep time: 5 minutes | Cook time: 7 minutes | Serves 4

24 frozen potato crunchies
6 slices cooked bacon
2 tablespoons maple syrup

240 ml shredded Cheddar cheese

1. Preheat the air fryer to 204ºC. 2. Put the potato crunchies in the air fryer basket. Air fry for 10 minutes, shaking the basket halfway through the cooking time. 3. Meanwhile, cut the bacon into 1-inch pieces. 4. Remove the potato crunchies from the air fryer basket and put into a baking pan. Top with the bacon and drizzle with the maple syrup. Air fry for 5 minutes, or until the crunchies and bacon are crisp. 5. Top with the cheese and air fry for 2 minutes, or until the cheese is melted. 6. Serve hot.

Cheesy Hash Brown Bruschetta

Prep time: 5 minutes | Cook time: 6 to 8 minutes | Serves 4

4 frozen hash brown patties
1 tablespoon olive oil
80 ml chopped cherry tomatoes
3 tablespoons diced fresh Mozzarella

2 tablespoons grated Parmesan cheese
1 tablespoon balsamic vinegar
1 tablespoon minced fresh basil

1. Preheat the air fryer to 204ºC. 2. Place the hash brown patties in the air fryer in a single layer. Air fry for 6 to 8 minutes, or until the potatoes are crisp, hot, and golden brown. 3. Meanwhile, combine the olive oil, tomatoes, Mozzarella, Parmesan, vinegar, and basil in a small bowl. 4. When the potatoes are done, carefully remove from the basket and arrange on a serving plate. Top with the tomato mixture and serve.

Crispy Breaded Beef Cubes

Prep time: 10 minutes | Cook time: 12 to 16 minutes | Serves 4

450 g sirloin tip, cut into 1-inch cubes
240 ml cheese pasta sauce

355 ml soft breadcrumbs
2 tablespoons olive oil
½ teaspoon dried marjoram

1. Preheat the air fryer to 182ºC. 2. In a medium bowl, toss the beef with the pasta sauce to coat. 3. In a shallow bowl, combine the breadcrumbs, oil, and marjoram, and mix well. Drop the beef cubes, one at a time, into the bread crumb mixture to coat thoroughly. 4. Air fry the beef in two batches for 6 to 8 minutes, shaking the basket once during cooking time, until the beef is at least 63ºC and the outside is crisp and brown. 5. Serve hot.

Poutine with Waffle Fries

Prep time: 10 minutes | Cook time: 15 to 17 minutes | Serves 4

475 ml frozen waffle cut fries
2 teaspoons olive oil
1 red pepper, chopped

2 spring onions, sliced
240 ml shredded Swiss cheese
120 ml bottled chicken gravy

1. Preheat the air fryer to 192ºC. 2. Toss the waffle fries with the olive oil and place in the air fryer basket. Air fry for 10 to 12 minutes, or until the fries are crisp and light golden brown, shaking the basket halfway through the cooking time. 3. Transfer the fries to a baking pan and top with the pepper, spring onions, and cheese. Air fry for 3 minutes, or until the vegetables are crisp and tender. 4. Remove the pan from the air fryer and drizzle the gravy over the fries. Air fry for 2 minutes, or until the gravy is hot. 5. Serve immediately.

Lemony Endive in Curried Yoghurt

Prep time: 5 minutes | Cook time: 10 minutes | Serves 6

6 heads endive
120 ml plain and fat-free yoghurt
3 tablespoons lemon juice

1 teaspoon garlic powder
½ teaspoon curry powder
Salt and ground black pepper, to taste

1. Wash the endives and slice them in half lengthwise. 2. In a bowl, mix together the yoghurt, lemon juice, garlic powder, curry powder, salt and pepper. 3. Brush the endive halves with the marinade, coating them completely. Allow to sit for at least 30 minutes or up to 24 hours. 4. Preheat the air fryer to 160ºC. 5. Put the endives in the air fryer basket and air fry for 10 minutes. 6. Serve hot.

Spicy Chicken Bites

Prep time: 10 minutes | Cook time: 10 to 12 minutes | Makes 30 bites

227 g boneless and skinless chicken thighs, cut into 30 pieces

¼ teaspoon rock salt
2 tablespoons hot sauce
Cooking spray

1. Preheat the air fryer to 200ºC. 2. Spray the air fryer basket with cooking spray and season the chicken bites with the rock salt, then place in the basket and air fry for 10 to 12 minutes or until crispy. 3. While the chicken bites cook, pour the hot sauce into a large bowl. 4. Remove the bites and add to the sauce bowl, tossing to coat. Serve warm.

Mozzarella Arancini

Prep time: 5 minutes | Cook time: 8 to 11 minutes | Makes 16 arancini

475 ml cooked rice, cooled
2 eggs, beaten
355 ml panko breadcrumbs, divided
120 ml grated Parmesan cheese
2 tablespoons minced fresh basil
16 ¾-inch cubes Mozzarella cheese
2 tablespoons olive oil

1. Preheat the air fryer to 204ºC. 2. In a medium bowl, combine the rice, eggs, 120 ml of the breadcrumbs, Parmesan cheese, and basil. Form this mixture into 16 1½-inch balls. 3. Poke a hole in each of the balls with your finger and insert a Mozzarella cube. Form the rice mixture firmly around the cheese. 4. On a shallow plate, combine the remaining 240 ml of the breadcrumbs with the olive oil and mix well. Roll the rice balls in the breadcrumbs to coat. 5. Air fry the arancini in batches for 8 to 11 minutes or until golden brown. 6. Serve hot.

Bruschetta with Basil Pesto

Prep time: 10 minutes | Cook time: 5 to 11 minutes | Serves 4

8 slices French bread, ½ inch thick
2 tablespoons softened butter
240 ml shredded Mozzarella cheese
120 ml basil pesto
240 ml chopped grape tomatoes
2 spring onions, thinly sliced

1. Preheat the air fryer to 176ºC. 2. Spread the bread with the butter and place butter-side up in the air fryer basket. Bake for 3 to 5 minutes, or until the bread is light golden brown. 3. Remove the bread from the basket and top each piece with some of the cheese. Return to the basket in 2 batches and bake for 1 to 3 minutes, or until the cheese melts. 4. Meanwhile, combine the pesto, tomatoes, and spring onions in a small bowl. 5. When the cheese has melted, remove the bread from the air fryer and place on a serving plate. Top each slice with some of the pesto mixture and serve.

Tortellini with Spicy Dipping Sauce

Prep time: 5 minutes | Cook time: 20 minutes | Serves 4

177 ml mayonnaise
2 tablespoons mustard
1 egg
120 ml flour
½ teaspoon dried oregano
355 ml breadcrumbs
2 tablespoons olive oil
475 ml frozen cheese tortellini

1. Preheat the air fryer to 192ºC. 2. In a small bowl, combine the mayonnaise and mustard and mix well. Set aside. 3. In a shallow bowl, beat the egg. In a separate bowl, combine the flour and oregano. In another bowl, combine the breadcrumbs and olive oil, and mix well. 4. Drop the tortellini, a few at a time, into the egg, then into the flour, then into the egg again, and then into the breadcrumbs to coat. Put into the air fryer basket, cooking in batches. 5. Air fry for about 10 minutes, shaking halfway through the cooking time, or until the tortellini are crisp and golden brown on the outside. Serve with the mayonnaise mixture.

Spinach and Crab Meat Cups

Prep time: 10 minutes | Cook time: 10 minutes | Makes 30 cups

1 (170 g) can crab meat, drained to yield 80 ml meat
60 ml frozen spinach, thawed, drained, and chopped
1 clove garlic, minced
120 ml grated Parmesan cheese
3 tablespoons plain yoghurt
¼ teaspoon lemon juice
½ teaspoon Worcestershire sauce
30 mini frozen filo shells, thawed
Cooking spray

1. Preheat the air fryer to 200ºC. 2. Remove any bits of shell that might remain in the crab meat. 3. Mix the crab meat, spinach, garlic, and cheese together. 4. Stir in the yoghurt, lemon juice, and Worcestershire sauce and mix well. 5. Spoon a teaspoon of filling into each filo shell. 6. Spray the air fryer basket with cooking spray and arrange half the shells in the basket. Air fry for 5 minutes. Repeat with the remaining shells. 7. Serve immediately.

Crispy Cajun Dill Pickle Chips

Prep time: 5 minutes | Cook time: 10 minutes | Makes 16 slices

60 ml plain flour
120 ml panko breadcrumbs
1 large egg, beaten
2 teaspoons Cajun seasoning
2 large dill pickles, sliced into 8 rounds each
Cooking spray

1. Preheat the air fryer to 200ºC. 2. Place the plain flour, panko breadcrumbs, and egg into 3 separate shallow bowls, then stir the Cajun seasoning into the flour. 3. Dredge each pickle chip in the flour mixture, then the egg, and finally the breadcrumbs. Shake off any excess, then place each coated pickle chip on a plate. 4. Spritz the air fryer basket with cooking spray, then place 8 pickle chips in the basket and air fry for 5 minutes, or until crispy and golden brown. Repeat this process with the remaining pickle chips. 5. Remove the chips and allow to slightly cool on a wire rack before serving.

Cheesy Steak Fries

Prep time: 5 minutes | Cook time: 20 minutes | Serves 5

1 (794 g) bag frozen steak fries

Cooking spray

Salt and pepper, to taste

120 ml beef gravy

240 ml shredded Mozzarella cheese

2 spring onions, green parts only, chopped

1. Preheat the air fryer to 204ºC. 2. Place the frozen steak fries in the air fryer. Air fry for 10 minutes. Shake the basket and spritz the fries with cooking spray. Sprinkle with salt and pepper. Air fry for an additional 8 minutes. 3. Pour the beef gravy into a medium, microwave-safe bowl. Microwave for 30 seconds, or until the gravy is warm. 4. Sprinkle the fries with the cheese. Air fry for an additional 2 minutes, until the cheese is melted. 5. Transfer the fries to a serving dish. Drizzle the fries with gravy and sprinkle the spring onions on top for a green garnish. Serve.

Chapter 9 Holiday Specials

Chapter 9 Holiday Specials

Whole Chicken Roast

Prep time: 10 minutes | Cook time: 1 hour | Serves 6

1 teaspoon salt	½ teaspoon garlic powder
1 teaspoon Italian seasoning	½ teaspoon onion powder
½ teaspoon freshly ground black pepper	2 tablespoons olive oil, plus more as needed
½ teaspoon paprika	1 (1.8 kg) small chicken

Preheat the air fryer to 182°C. Grease the air fryer basket lightly with olive oil. In a small bowl, mix the salt, Italian seasoning, pepper, paprika, garlic powder, and onion powder. Remove any giblets from the chicken. Pat the chicken dry thoroughly with paper towels, including the cavity. Brush the chicken all over with the olive oil and rub it with the seasoning mixture. Truss the chicken or tie the legs with butcher's twine. This will make it easier to flip the chicken during cooking. Put the chicken in the air fryer basket, breast-side down. Air fry for 30 minutes. Flip the chicken over and baste it with any drippings collected in the bottom drawer of the air fryer. Lightly brush the chicken with olive oil. Air fry for 20 minutes. Flip the chicken over one last time and air fry until a thermometer inserted into the thickest part of the thigh reaches at least 74°C and it's crispy and golden, 10 more minutes. Continue to cook, checking every 5 minutes until the chicken reaches the correct internal temperature. Let the chicken rest for 10 minutes before carving and serving.

Lush Snack Mix

Prep time: 10 minutes | Cook time: 10 minutes | Serves 10

120 ml honey	475 ml granola
3 tablespoons butter, melted	235 ml cashews
1 teaspoon salt	475 ml crispy corn puff cereal
475 ml sesame sticks	475 ml mini pretzel crisps
475 ml pumpkin seeds	

In a bowl, combine the honey, butter, and salt. In another bowl, mix the sesame sticks, pumpkin seeds, granola, cashews, corn puff cereal, and pretzel crisps. Combine the contents of the two bowls. Preheat the air fryer to 188°C. Put the mixture in the air fryer basket and air fry for 10 to 12 minutes to toast the snack mixture, shaking the basket frequently. Do this in two batches. Put the snack mix on a cookie sheet and allow it to cool fully. Serve immediately.

Eggnog Bread

Prep time: 10 minutes | Cook time: 18 minutes | Serves 6 to 8

235 ml flour, plus more for dusting	1 tablespoon plus 1 teaspoon butter, melted
60 ml sugar	60 ml pecans
1 teaspoon baking powder	60 ml chopped candied fruit (cherries, pineapple, or mixed fruits)
¼ teaspoon salt	
¼ teaspoon nutmeg	
120 ml eggnog	Cooking spray
1 egg yolk	

Preheat the air fryer to 182°C. In a medium bowl, stir together the flour, sugar, baking powder, salt, and nutmeg. Add eggnog, egg yolk, and butter. Mix well but do not beat. Stir in nuts and fruit. Spray a baking pan with cooking spray and dust with flour. Spread batter into prepared pan and bake for 18 minutes or until top is dark golden brown and bread starts to pull away from sides of pan. Serve immediately.

Mushroom and Green Bean Casserole

Prep time: 10 minutes | Cook time: 15 minutes | Serves 4

4 tablespoons unsalted butter	120 ml chicken broth
60 ml diced brown onion	¼ teaspoon xanthan gum
120 ml chopped white mushrooms	450 g fresh green beans, edges trimmed
120 ml double cream	14 g pork crackling, finely ground
30 g full fat soft white cheese	

In a medium skillet over medium heat, melt the butter. Sauté the onion and mushrooms until they become soft and fragrant, about 3 to 5 minutes. Add the double cream, soft white cheese, and broth to the pan. Whisk until smooth. Bring to a boil and then reduce to a simmer. Sprinkle the xanthan gum into the pan and remove from heat. Preheat the air fryer to 160°C. Chop the green beans into 2-inch pieces and place into a baking dish. Pour the sauce mixture over them and stir until coated. Top the dish with minced pork crackling. Put into the air fryer basket and bake for 15 minutes. Top will be golden and green beans fork-tender when fully cooked. Serve warm.

Hearty Honey Yeast Rolls

Prep time: 10 minutes | Cook time: 20 minutes | Makes 8 rolls

60 ml whole milk, heated to 46°C in the microwave
½ teaspoon active dry yeast
1 tablespoon honey
160 ml plain flour, plus more for dusting

½ teaspoon rock salt
2 tablespoons unsalted butter, at room temperature, plus more for greasing
Flaky sea salt, to taste

In a large bowl, whisk together the milk, yeast, and honey and let stand until foamy, about 10 minutes. Stir in the flour and salt until just combined. Stir in the butter until absorbed. Scrape the dough onto a lightly floured work surface and knead until smooth, about 6 minutes. Transfer the dough to a lightly greased bowl, cover loosely with a sheet of plastic wrap or a kitchen towel, and let sit until nearly doubled in size, about 1 hour. Uncover the dough, lightly press it down to expel the bubbles, then portion it into 8 equal pieces. Prep the work surface by wiping it clean with a damp paper towel (if there is flour on the work surface, it will prevent the dough from sticking lightly to the surface, which helps it form a ball). Roll each piece into a ball by cupping the palm of the hand around the dough against the work surface and moving the heel of the hand in a circular motion while using the thumb to contain the dough and tighten it into a perfectly round ball. Once all the balls are formed, nestle them side by side in the air fryer basket. Cover the rolls loosely with a kitchen towel or a sheet of plastic wrap and let sit until lightly risen and puffed, 20 to 30 minutes. Preheat the air fryer to 132°C. Uncover the rolls and gently brush with more butter, being careful not to press the rolls too hard. Air fry until the rolls are light golden brown and fluffy, about 12 minutes. Remove the rolls from the air fryer and brush liberally with more butter, if you like, and sprinkle each roll with a pinch of sea salt. Serve warm.

Air Fried Blistered Tomatoes

Prep time: 5 minutes | Cook time: 10 minutes | Serves 4 to 6

900 g cherry tomatoes
2 tablespoons olive oil
2 teaspoons balsamic vinegar

½ teaspoon salt
½ teaspoon ground black pepper

Preheat the air fryer with a cake pan to 204°C. Toss the cherry tomatoes with olive oil in a large bowl to coat well. Pour the tomatoes in the cake pan. Air fry the cherry tomatoes for 10 minutes or until the tomatoes are blistered and lightly wilted. Shake the basket halfway through. Transfer the blistered tomatoes to a large bowl and toss with balsamic vinegar, salt, and black pepper before serving.

Cinnamon Rolls with Cream Glaze

Prep time: 2 hours 15 minutes | Cook time: 10 minutes | Serves 8

450 g frozen bread dough, thawed
2 tablespoons melted butter
1½ tablespoons cinnamon
180 ml brown sugar
Cooking spray

Cream Glaze:
110 g soft white cheese
½ teaspoon vanilla extract
2 tablespoons melted butter
300 ml powdered erythritol

Place the bread dough on a clean work surface, then roll the dough out into a rectangle with a rolling pin. Brush the top of the dough with melted butter and leave 1-inch edges uncovered. Combine the cinnamon and sugar in a small bowl, then sprinkle the dough with the cinnamon mixture. Roll the dough over tightly, then cut the dough log into 8 portions. Wrap the portions in plastic, better separately, and let sit to rise for 1 or 2 hours. Meanwhile, combine the ingredients for the glaze in a separate small bowl. Stir to mix well. Preheat the air fryer to 176°C. Spritz the air fryer basket with cooking spray. Transfer the risen rolls to the preheated air fryer. You may need to work in batches to avoid overcrowding. Air fry for 5 minutes or until golden brown. Flip the rolls halfway through. Serve the rolls with the glaze.

Classic Churros

Prep time: 35 minutes | Cook time: 10 minutes per batch | Makes 12 churros

4 tablespoons butter
¼ teaspoon salt
120 ml water
120 ml plain flour

2 large eggs
2 teaspoons ground cinnamon
60 ml granulated white sugar
Cooking spray

Put the butter, salt, and water in a saucepan. Bring to a boil until the butter is melted on high heat. Keep stirring. Reduce the heat to medium and fold in the flour to form a dough. Keep cooking and stirring until the dough is dried out and coat the pan with a crust. Turn off the heat and scrape the dough in a large bowl. Allow to cool for 15 minutes. Break and whisk the eggs into the dough with a hand mixer until the dough is sanity and firm enough to shape. Scoop up 1 tablespoon of the dough and roll it into a ½-inch-diameter and 2-inch-long cylinder. Repeat with remaining dough to make 12 cylinders in total. Combine the cinnamon and sugar in a large bowl and dunk the cylinders into the cinnamon mix to coat. Arrange the cylinders on a plate and refrigerate for 20 minutes. Preheat the air fryer to 192°C. Spritz the air fryer basket with cooking spray. Place the cylinders in batches in the air fryer basket and spritz with cooking spray. Air fry for 10 minutes or until golden brown and fluffy. Flip them halfway through. Serve immediately.

Kale Salad Sushi Rolls with Sriracha Mayonnaise

Prep time: 10 minutes | Cook time: 10 minutes | Serves 12

Kale Salad:
350 ml chopped kale
1 tablespoon sesame seeds
¾ teaspoon soy sauce
¾ teaspoon toasted sesame oil
½ teaspoon rice vinegar
¼ teaspoon ginger
⅛ teaspoon garlic powder
Sushi Rolls:

3 sheets sushi nori
1 batch cauliflower rice
½ avocado, sliced
Sriracha Mayonnaise:
60 ml Sriracha sauce
60 ml vegan mayonnaise
Coating:
120 ml panko breadcrumbs

Preheat the air fryer to 200ºC. In a medium bowl, toss all the ingredients for the salad together until well coated and set aside. Place a sheet of nori on a clean work surface and spread the cauliflower rice in an even layer on the nori. Scoop 2 to 3 tablespoon of kale salad on the rice and spread over. Place 1 or 2 avocado slices on top. Roll up the sushi, pressing gently to get a nice, tight roll. Repeat to make the remaining 2 rolls. In a bowl, stir together the Sriracha sauce and mayonnaise until smooth. Add breadcrumbs to a separate bowl. Dredge the sushi rolls in Sriracha Mayonnaise, then roll in breadcrumbs till well coated. Place the coated sushi rolls in the air fryer basket and air fry for 10 minutes, or until golden brown and crispy. Flip the sushi rolls gently halfway through to ensure even cooking. Transfer to a platter and rest for 5 minutes before slicing each roll into 8 pieces. Serve warm.

Arancini

Prep time: 5 minutes | Cook time: 30 minutes | Makes 10 arancini

160 ml raw white Arborio rice
2 teaspoons butter
½ teaspoon salt
315 ml water
2 large eggs, well beaten
300 ml dried breadcrumbs

mixed with Italian-style seasoning
10 ¾-inch semi-firm Mozzarella cubes
Cooking spray

Pour the rice, butter, salt, and water in a pot. Stir to mix well and bring a boil over medium-high heat. Keep stirring. Reduce the heat to low and cover the pot. Simmer for 20 minutes or until the rice is tender. Turn off the heat and let sit, covered, for 10 minutes, then open the lid and fluffy the rice with a fork. Allow to cool for 10 more minutes. Preheat the air fryer to 192ºC. Pour the beaten eggs in a bowl, then pour the breadcrumbs in a separate bowl. Scoop 2 tablespoons of the cooked rice up and form it into a ball, then press the Mozzarella into the ball and wrap. Dredge the ball in the eggs first, then shake the excess off the dunk the ball in the breadcrumbs.

Roll to coat evenly. Repeat to make 10 balls in total with remaining rice. Transfer the balls in the preheated air fryer and spritz with cooking spray. You need to work in batches to avoid overcrowding. Air fry for 10 minutes or until the balls are lightly browned and crispy. Remove the balls from the air fryer and allow to cool before serving.

Air Fried Spicy Olives

Prep time: 10 minutes | Cook time: 5 minutes | Serves 4

340 g pitted black extra-large olives
60 ml plain flour
235 ml panko breadcrumbs
2 teaspoons dried thyme

1 teaspoon red pepper flakes
1 teaspoon smoked paprika
1 egg beaten with 1 tablespoon water
Vegetable oil for spraying

Preheat the air fryer to 204ºC. Drain the olives and place them on a paper towel–lined plate to dry. Put the flour on a plate. Combine the panko, thyme, red pepper flakes, and paprika on a separate plate. Dip an olive in the flour, shaking off any excess, then coat with egg mixture. Dredge the olive in the panko mixture, pressing to make the crumbs adhere, and place the breaded olive on a platter. Repeat with the remaining olives. Spray the olives with oil and place them in a single layer in the air fryer basket. Work in batches if necessary so as not to overcrowd the basket. Air fry for 5 minutes until the breading is browned and crispy. Serve warm

Simple Butter Cake

Prep time: 25 minutes | Cook time: 20 minutes | Serves 8

235 ml plain flour
1¼ teaspoons baking powder
¼ teaspoon salt
120 ml plus 1½ tablespoons granulated white sugar
9½ tablespoons butter, at room

temperature
2 large eggs
1 large egg yolk
2½ tablespoons milk
1 teaspoon vanilla extract
Cooking spray

Preheat the air fryer to 164ºC. Spritz a cake pan with cooking spray. Combine the flour, baking powder, and salt in a large bowl. Stir to mix well. Whip the sugar and butter in a separate bowl with a hand mixer on medium speed for 3 minutes. Whip the eggs, egg yolk, milk, and vanilla extract into the sugar and butter mix with a hand mixer. Pour in the flour mixture and whip with hand mixer until sanity and smooth. Scrape the batter into the cake pan and level the batter with a spatula. Place the cake pan in the preheated air fryer. Bake for 20 minutes or until a toothpick inserted in the centre comes out clean. Check the doneness during the last 5 minutes of the baking. Invert the cake on a cooling rack and allow to cool for 15 minutes before slicing to serve.

Shrimp with Sriracha and Worcestershire Sauce

Prep time: 15 minutes | Cook time: 10 minutes per batch | Serves 4

1 tablespoon Sriracha sauce	235 ml panko breadcrumbs
1 teaspoon Worcestershire sauce	450 g raw shrimp, shelled and
2 tablespoons sweet chilli sauce	deveined, rinsed and drained
180 ml mayonnaise	Lime wedges, for serving
1 egg, beaten	Cooking spray

Preheat the air fryer to 182°C. Spritz the air fryer basket with cooking spray. Combine the Sriracha sauce, Worcestershire sauce, chilli sauce, and mayo in a bowl. Stir to mix well. Reserve 80 ml the mixture as the dipping sauce. Combine the remaining sauce mixture with the beaten egg. Stir to mix well. Put the panko in a separate bowl. Dredge the shrimp in the sauce mixture first, then into the panko. Roll the shrimp to coat well. Shake the excess off. Place the shrimp in the preheated air fryer, then spritz with cooking spray. You may need to work in batches to avoid overcrowding. Air fry the shrimp for 10 minutes or until opaque. Flip the shrimp halfway through the cooking time. Remove the shrimp from the air fryer and serve with reserve sauce mixture and squeeze the lime wedges over.

Supplì al Telefono (Risotto Croquettes)

Prep time: 1 hour 40 minutes | Cook time: 1 hour | Serves 6

Risotto Croquettes:	Rock salt and ground black
4 tablespoons unsalted butter	pepper, to taste
1 small brown onion, minced	Cooking spray
235 ml Arborio rice	Tomato Sauce:
820 ml chicken stock	2 tablespoons extra-virgin olive
120 ml dry white wine	oil
3 eggs	4 cloves garlic, minced
Zest of 1 lemon	¼ teaspoon red pepper flakes
120 ml grated Parmesan cheese	1 (794 g) can crushed tomatoes
60 g fresh Mozzarella cheese	or passata
60 ml peas	2 teaspoons granulated sugar
2 tablespoons water	Rock salt and ground black
120 ml plain flour	pepper, to taste
350 ml panko breadcrumbs	

Melt the butter in a pot over medium heat, then add the onion and salt to taste. Sauté for 5 minutes or until the onion is translucent. Add the rice and stir to coat well. Cook for 3 minutes or until the rice is lightly browned. Pour in the chicken stock and wine. Bring to a boil. Then cook for 20 minutes or until the rice is tender and liquid is almost absorbed. Make the risotto: When the rice is cooked, break the egg into the pot. Add the lemon zest and

Parmesan cheese. Sprinkle with salt and ground black pepper. Stir to mix well. Pour the risotto in a baking sheet, then level with a spatula to spread the risotto evenly. Wrap the baking sheet in plastic and refrigerate for1 hour. Meanwhile, heat the olive oil in a saucepan over medium heat until shimmering. Add the garlic and sprinkle with red pepper flakes. Sauté for a minute or until fragrant. Add the crushed tomatoes and sprinkle with sugar. Stir to mix well. Bring to a boil. Reduce the heat to low and simmer for 15 minutes or until lightly thickened. Sprinkle with salt and pepper to taste. Set aside until ready to serve. Remove the risotto from the refrigerator. Scoop the risotto into twelve 2-inch balls, then flatten the balls with your hands. Arrange a about ½-inch piece of Mozzarella and 5 peas in the centre of each flattened ball, then wrap them back into balls. Transfer the balls in a baking sheet lined with parchment paper, then refrigerate for 15 minutes or until firm. Preheat the air fryer to 204°C. Whisk the remaining 2 eggs with 2 tablespoons of water in a bowl. Pour the flour in a second bowl and pour the panko in a third bowl. Dredge the risotto balls in the bowl of flour first, then into the eggs, and then into the panko. Shake the excess off. Transfer the balls in the preheated air fryer and spritz with cooking spray. You may need to work in batches to avoid overcrowding. Bake for 10 minutes or until golden brown. Flip the balls halfway through. Serve the risotto balls with the tomato sauce.

Fried Dill Pickles with Buttermilk Dressing

Prep time: 45 minutes | Cook time: 8 minutes | Serves 6 to 8

Buttermilk Dressing:	pepper, to taste
60 ml buttermilk	Fried Dill Pickles:
60 ml chopped spring onions	180 ml plain flour
180 ml mayonnaise	1 (900 g) jar kosher dill pickles,
120 ml sour cream	cut into 4 spears, drained
½ teaspoon cayenne pepper	600 ml panko breadcrumbs
½ teaspoon onion powder	2 eggs, beaten with 2
½ teaspoon garlic powder	tablespoons water
1 tablespoon chopped chives	Rock salt and ground black
2 tablespoons chopped fresh dill	pepper, to taste
Rock salt and ground black	Cooking spray

Preheat the air fryer to 204°C. Combine the ingredients for the dressing in a bowl. Stir to mix well. Wrap the bowl in plastic and refrigerate for 30 minutes or until ready to serve. Pour the flour in a bowl and sprinkle with salt and ground black pepper. Stir to mix well. Put the breadcrumbs in a separate bowl. Pour the beaten eggs in a third bowl. Dredge the pickle spears in the flour, then into the eggs, and then into the panko to coat well. Shake the excess off. Arrange the pickle spears in a single layer in the preheated air fryer and spritz with cooking spray. Air fry for 8 minutes. Flip the pickle spears halfway through. Serve the pickle spears with buttermilk dressing.

Garlicky Olive Stromboli

Prep time: 25 minutes | Cook time: 25 minutes | Serves 8

4 large cloves garlic, unpeeled	¼ teaspoon crushed red pepper
3 tablespoons grated Parmesan cheese	230 g pizza dough, at room temperature
120 ml packed fresh basil leaves	110 g sliced provolone cheese (about 8 slices)
120 ml marinated, pitted green and black olives	Cooking spray

Preheat the air fryer to 188°C. Spritz the air fryer basket with cooking spray. Put the unpeeled garlic in the air fryer basket. Air fry for 10 minutes or until the garlic is softened completely. Remove them from the air fryer and allow to cool until you can handle. Peel the garlic and place into a food processor with 2 tablespoons of Parmesan, basil, olives, and crushed red pepper. Pulse to mix well. Set aside. Arrange the pizza dough on a clean work surface, then roll it out with a rolling pin into a rectangle. Cut the rectangle in half. Sprinkle half of the garlic mixture over each rectangle half and leave ½-inch edges uncover. Top them with the provolone cheese. Brush one long side of each rectangle half with water, then roll them up. Spritz the air fryer basket with cooking spray. Transfer the rolls in the preheated air fryer. Spritz with cooking spray and scatter with remaining Parmesan. Air fry the rolls for 15 minutes or until golden brown. Flip the rolls halfway through. Remove the rolls from the air fryer and allow to cool for a few minutes before serving.

Jewish Blintzes

Prep time: 5 minutes | Cook time: 10 minutes | Makes 8 blintzes

2 (213 g) packages farmer or ricotta cheese, mashed	60 ml granulated white sugar
60 ml soft white cheese	8 egg roll wrappers
¼ teaspoon vanilla extract	4 tablespoons butter, melted

Preheat the air fryer to 192°C. Combine the cheese, soft white cheese, vanilla extract, and sugar in a bowl. Stir to mix well. Unfold the egg roll wrappers on a clean work surface, spread 60 ml filling at the edge of each wrapper and leave a ½-inch edge uncovering. Wet the edges of the wrappers with water and fold the uncovered edge over the filling. Fold the left and right sides in the centre, then tuck the edge under the filling and fold to wrap the filling. Brush the wrappers with melted butter, then arrange the wrappers in a single layer in the preheated air fryer, seam side down. Leave a little space between each two wrappers. Work in batches to avoid overcrowding. Air fry for 10 minutes or until golden brown. Serve immediately.

Golden Nuggets

Prep time: 15 minutes | Cook time: 4 minutes per batch | Makes 20 nuggets

235 ml plain flour, plus more for dusting	¼ teaspoon salt
1 teaspoon baking powder	60 ml water
½ teaspoon butter, at room temperature, plus more for brushing	⅛ teaspoon onion powder
	¼ teaspoon garlic powder
	⅛ teaspoon seasoning salt
	Cooking spray

Preheat the air fryer to 188°C. Line the air fryer basket with parchment paper. Mix the flour, baking powder, butter, and salt in a large bowl. Stir to mix well. Gradually whisk in the water until a sanity dough forms. Put the dough on a lightly floured work surface, then roll it out into a ½-inch thick rectangle with a rolling pin. Cut the dough into about twenty 1- or 2-inch squares, then arrange the squares in a single layer in the preheated air fryer. Spritz with cooking spray. You need to work in batches to avoid overcrowding. Combine onion powder, garlic powder, and seasoning salt in a small bowl. Stir to mix well, then sprinkle the squares with the powder mixture. Air fry the dough squares for 4 minutes or until golden brown. Flip the squares halfway through the cooking time. Remove the golden nuggets from the air fryer and brush with more butter immediately. Serve warm.

Teriyaki Shrimp Skewers

Prep time: 10 minutes | Cook time: 6 minutes | Makes 12 skewered shrimp

1½ tablespoons mirin	deveined
1½ teaspoons ginger paste	1 large egg
1½ tablespoons soy sauce	180 ml panko breadcrumbs
12 large shrimp, peeled and	Cooking spray

Combine the mirin, ginger paste, and soy sauce in a large bowl. Stir to mix well. Dunk the shrimp in the bowl of mirin mixture, then wrap the bowl in plastic and refrigerate for 1 hour to marinate. Preheat the air fryer to 204°C. Spritz the air fryer basket with cooking spray. Run twelve 4-inch skewers through each shrimp. Whisk the egg in the bowl of marinade to combine well. Pour the breadcrumbs on a plate. Dredge the shrimp skewers in the egg mixture, then shake the excess off and roll over the breadcrumbs to coat well. Arrange the shrimp skewers in the preheated air fryer and spritz with cooking spray. You need to work in batches to avoid overcrowding. Air fry for 6 minutes or until the shrimp are opaque and firm. Flip the shrimp skewers halfway through. Serve immediately.

Hasselback Potatoes

Prep time: 5 minutes | Cook time: 50 minutes | Serves 4

4 russet or Maris Piper potatoes, peeled

Salt and freshly ground black

pepper, to taste

60 ml grated Parmesan cheese

Cooking spray

Preheat the air fryer to 204°C. Spray the air fryer basket lightly with cooking spray. Make thin parallel cuts into each potato, ⅛-inch to ¼-inch apart, stopping at about ½ of the way through. The potato needs to stay intact along the bottom. Spray the potatoes with cooking spray and use the hands or a silicone brush to completely coat the potatoes lightly in oil. Put the potatoes, sliced side up, in the air fryer basket in a single layer. Leave a little room between each potato. Sprinkle the potatoes lightly with salt and black pepper. Air fry for 20 minutes. Reposition the potatoes and spritz lightly with cooking spray again. Air fry until the potatoes are fork-tender and crispy and browned, another 20 to 30 minutes. Sprinkle the potatoes with Parmesan cheese and serve.

Mexican Pizza

Prep time: 10 minutes | Cook time: 7 to 9 minutes | Serves 4

180 ml refried beans

120 ml salsa

10 frozen precooked beef meatballs, thawed and sliced

1 jalapeño pepper, sliced

4 wholemeal pitta breads

235 ml shredded pepper Jack or Monterey Jack cheese

120 ml shredded Colby or Gouda cheese

80 ml sour cream

In a medium bowl, combine the refried beans, salsa, meatballs, and jalapeño pepper. Preheat the air fryer for 3 to 4 minutes or until hot. Top the pittas with the refried bean mixture and sprinkle with the cheeses. Bake at 188°C for 7 to 9 minutes or until the pizza is crisp and the cheese is melted and starts to brown. Top each pizza with a dollop of sour cream and serve warm.

Custard Donut Holes with Chocolate Glaze

Prep time: 1 hour 50 minutes | Cook time: 4 minutes per batch | Makes 24 donut holes

Dough:

350 ml bread flour

2 egg yolks

1 teaspoon active dry yeast

120 ml warm milk

½ teaspoon pure vanilla extract

2 tablespoons butter, melted

1 tablespoon sugar

¼ teaspoon salt

Cooking spray

Custard Filling:

1 (96 g) box French vanilla instant pudding mix

60 ml double cream

180 ml whole milk

Chocolate Glaze:

80 ml double cream

235 ml chocolate chips

Special Equipment:

A pastry bag with a long tip

Combine the ingredients for the dough in a food processor, then pulse until a satiny dough ball forms. Transfer the dough on a lightly floured work surface, then knead for 2 minutes by hand and shape the dough back to a ball. Spritz a large bowl with cooking spray, then transfer the dough ball into the bowl. Wrap the bowl in plastic and let it rise for 1½ hours or until it doubled in size. Transfer the risen dough on a floured work surface, then shape it into a 24-inch-long log. Cut the log into 24 parts and shape each part into a ball. Transfer the balls on two or three baking sheets and let sit to rise for 30 more minutes. Preheat the air fryer to 204°C. Arrange the baking sheets in the air fryer. You need to work in batches to avoid overcrowding. Spritz the balls with cooking spray. Bake for 4 minutes or until golden brown. Flip the balls halfway through. Meanwhile, combine the ingredients for the filling in a large bowl and whisk for 2 minutes with a hand mixer until well combined. Pour the double cream in a saucepan, then bring to a boil. Put the chocolate chips in a small bowl and pour in the boiled double cream immediately. Mix until the chocolate chips are melted, and the mixture is smooth. Transfer the baked donut holes to a large plate, then pierce a hole into each donut hole and lightly hollow them. Pour the filling in a pastry bag with a long tip and gently squeeze the filling into the donut holes. Then top the donut holes with chocolate glaze. Allow to sit for 10 minutes, then serve.

Printed in Great Britain
by Amazon

86752573R00047